Willing Hands 2

MORE COUNTED THREAD EMBROIDERY BY BETSY MORGAN

She seeketh wool and flax
and worketh willingly with her hands.

Proverbs 31:13

INSPIRATIONS

introduction

MANY YEARS AGO, a student suggested that, when I retired, I should publish a book of my designs. I thought it was a great idea and gave it some consideration but then put it aside as I had no idea how to even begin the process.

Enter Inspirations Studios who, in 2018, approached me about doing that very thing. To say that I was enthusiastic would be a monumental understatement! Who better to put together a book that would not only be informative but would be absolutely beautiful? They took a challenge which I had thought insurmountable and made it a gorgeous success while also making it look easy.

The success of my first Willing Hands floored me! The response from readers and former students was wonderful and humbling. I have received feedback from stitchers all over the world and all of it has been positive. I have even heard from some who have never stitched before but have been inspired by the book to give it a try! What more could anyone ask?

When, in the middle of the pandemic last year, Inspirations approached me about doing a second volume I was hesitant at first. My concern was that a sequel is rarely as good as the original. However, my husband convinced me that I should do it for my students, for those who were never able to take one of my classes, and for those who have read, enjoyed and stitched from the first book.

In Willing Hands 2 I have chosen a range of projects, some quite simple designs for those with less stitching and construction experience, and some that are more challenging.

Although I am now retired, it seems as if I'm busier than ever. When I look back at my 20-year career of designing and teaching, I am still amazed that it happened at all. This was not part of my original life plan, but with the guidance, enthusiasm and support of uncounted people, it became a glorious adventure! To all of you who have taken my classes, enjoyed the projects published in Inspirations magazine and Willing Hands Volume 1, and have kept in touch with me over the years, you have my thanks, from the bottom of my heart.

It has been a great experience and would never have happened without you!

BETSY MORGAN

contents

general information

FABRIC

All embroidery designs featured in this book are worked on 32-count linen. When making any of these projects, ensure your linen is 32-count for best results. The embroidered panels will be smaller if a higher count linen is used, and larger if a smaller count linen is used. To check the count of a piece of linen, place two pins 2.5cm (1") apart in the fabric and count the number of parallel threads between them. For 32-count linen, there should be 32 fabric threads. The number of threads should be the same for both the warp and weft. Note that this applies to counted embroidery linen rather than linen in general.

"Linen is not very consistent, and one cannot always depend on 32-count linen to actually be 32-count, in either warp or weft. The measurements given in the instructions are based on the measurements from my own stitched models, but they may not always work for others, due to those inconsistencies and due to the tension of individual stitchers. So, it is very important to use the measurements as an approximate starting point and to adjust yours as needed.

For the same reason, it is also very important to follow the linen layouts for each design, being sure not to turn any of the stitched areas by 90 degrees.

I prefer to work on linen which has a lot of sizing in it, though I frequently use Belfast linen which does not have much sizing. Some designers will suggest washing to remove the sizing, but that can shrink the linen."

THREADS

Although any stranded silk, cotton or rayon threads can be used, be aware that variegated colours create more interest in the designs, and silk and rayon threads will be more lustrous.

"All of my designs use Gloriana 12 ply hand-dyed silk thread. Even the monochromatic threads are variegated to some extent and I think that variegation gives more depth to my embroidery. Because of the variegation, it is very important to work each stitch in its entirety before moving on to the next. If you stitch a row of cross stitches in two linear journeys, you will get a "tweedy" effect rather than a lovely flow of change in colour or shade. No matter what fibre I am using, I never work my rows of stitches in journeys.

I am frequently asked if one should use one or two strands of embroidery thread in the needle for working my designs. I usually use one because I'm not concerned about coverage and I like to see the various legs of a stitch rather than a block of colour. I also like the lacier effect and don't like the bulkiness of using more than one strand. But that is my preference; feel free to follow your own."

NEEDLES

Tapestry needles are used to stitch counted thread techniques as the blunt tip slides easily between the fabric threads without splitting them. The large eye also makes them easy to thread. Choose good quality needles with a straight, smooth shaft and clean eye.

"We all know that there are numerous types of needles and it is important to use the correct one for each fabric or technique when constructing my designs. My rule of thumb is to use a tapestry needle and perlé cotton when sewing linen to linen, and a sewing needle (I prefer a milliner's needle) and sewing or beading thread when sewing linen to the lining fabric or pieces of the lining fabric to each other."

INTERLINING

Also known as buckram, interlining is a non-woven stiffener that is used in the production of soft furnishings. It is manufactured under the *Skirtex* label in the US. When constructing the Bee Contained Etui the interlining is scored to enable it to bend to shape. Use a ruler and craft knife to lightly score where indicated and bend one side away from the scoring.

"It should bend into a clean fold. If not, you may need to score the lines again but use a light touch – you don't want to cut all the way through."

FRAME OR HAND?

All the projects included in this book can be worked in the hand or in a frame. The dimensions given for the linen for each etui have been calculated for working in the hand. If you would prefer to use a frame, you may need additional linen along each edge to attach the fabric. Purchase a larger piece of linen or, alternatively, sew strips of calico (muslin) along each edge of the linen to enlarge the piece and attach these extensions to your frame.

"I use either stretcher bars or a scroll frame for all my linen projects because of limitations with my hands. I only use hoops for stumpwork and other surface embroidery, but never for linen. It is very difficult to remove creases or hoop marks from linen and I never wet my needlework once it is complete. Gloriana threads and some of the linens I use are not colourfast, so using water or ironing sprays to help iron out creases is out of the question. Keeping your hands and your work clean is essential."

CONSTRUCTION

When cutting out and constructing the etuis and accessories, the seam allowance is 13mm (½") unless specified. When stitching panels together for smaller accessories, such as scissor fobs, you may prefer to trim the seam allowance further to remove excess fabric and reduce bulk.

"Make sure that you clean up the back of your stitching before fusing the lightweight interfacing in place. Trim away any thread ends that may show through."

bee contained etui

This design was inspired by Stasi Buhrman, an avid and talented stitcher and friend of mine for many years.

WE HAVE KNOWN EACH OTHER through the Loudoun Sampler Guild in Leesburg, Virginia and also through my annual classes at Salty Yarns in Ocean City, Maryland.

Stasi is the Queen of Bees and adores everything apian. She has a fun blog called Bee-mused and Bee-stitching where she documents not only her own needlework but that of friends. It is one of a handful of stitcher's blogs that I follow regularly and, unlike me, she actually blogs on a regular basis.

Stasi's love of bees has infected me and I now can't look at anything bee related without thinking of her. So, Stasi, thanks for the inspiration, not only for this design, but for all your lovely needlework! And for the years of friendship!

this design uses

Back stitch

Cross stitch

Diamond eyelet

Double running stitch

Four-sided stitch

Long-arm cross stitch

Satin stitch

before you begin

See page 163 for the alphabet and number chart

We recommend that you read the complete article and construction information

All embroidery is worked with ONE strand of thread

The finished etui measures 9.5cm x 12.5cm wide (3¾" x 5").

requirements

Fabric

46cm x 33cm wide (18" x 13") piece of pale yellow 32-count linen

60cm x 30cm wide (24" x 12") piece of black silk dupion

Supplies

5cm x 50cm wide (2" x 20") piece of gold wool felt

25cm (10") square of lightweight fusible interfacing

23cm x 30cm wide (9" x 12") piece of interlining

28cm x 21.5cm wide (11" x 8½") sheets of comic board or firm card (2)

3cm x 2.5cm diameter (1¼" x 1") plastic or card cylinder*

Contrasting sewing thread

Black beading thread

11mm (⅜") hexagon mother-of-pearl buttons (2)

Susan Clark Originals charms:

BE-105 2.5cm x 3.5cm wide (1" x 1⅜") large bee button

BE-201 8mm x 10mm wide (⁵⁄₁₆" x ⅜") small bee button

C-1432 2cm x 2.5cm wide (¾" x 1") queen bee charm

C-1588 1.5cm (⅝") square beehive charm

SD-171 1cm x 1.5cm wide (⅜" x ⅝") sew-down bee

Ruler

Craft knife

4.5cm x 6cm wide (1¾" x 2⅜") piece of firm card

Fine heat-soluble fabric marker

Needles

No. 10 milliner's

No. 24 tapestry

No. 26 tapestry

Threads

DMC no. 12 perlé cotton

A = 310 black

B = 676 lt old gold

Gloriana stranded silk

C = 207 Inca gold

D = 211 antique black

Gloriana 7mm silk ribbon

E = 211 antique black – 45cm (18")

*Betsy used the plastic cylinder from the centre of a ball of perlé cotton

preparation for embroidery

PREPARING THE FABRIC

Neaten the edges of the linen with a machine zigzag or overlock stitch to prevent fraying.

TRANSFERRING THE DESIGN

Work all tacking lines along the grainlines using the contrasting thread. At the upper left-hand corner of the linen rectangle measure in and mark 5cm (2") from the upper edge and 4cm (1½") from the side edge. Beginning at this point and working over and under four threads, mark out each piece following the diagram (diag 1).

NOTE On each vertical side of the needlebook there is a compensating stitch worked over six threads. Work under or over six threads at this point. On the diagonal edges of the thread winder there are compensating stitches worked over two threads. Work under or over two threads at these points.

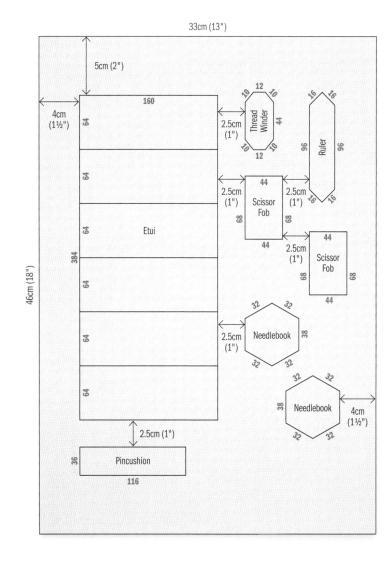

embroidery

Refer to the charts and close-up photographs for colour and stitch placement.

Use the no. 26 tapestry needle for all embroidery and the no. 10 milliner's needle and no. 24 tapestry for constructing the etui.

All embroidery is worked in the hand.

Each square on each graph represents 2 x 2 fabric threads.

ORDER OF WORK

All stitches are worked over two threads unless specified. On each panel work the back stitch lines over four threads using **A**. Remove the tacking threads as you work. On the needlebook take care to work the compensating stitches on each vertical side over six stitches. On the thread winder panels take care to work the compensating stitches on the diagonal edges over two stitches.

HINT *When working cross stitch with variegated threads complete each cross before moving on to the next.*

ETUI

Embroider the honeycomb border in double running stitch using **C**.

Panels 1 and 4: Work the skeps with double running stitch and the bee wings with back stitch using **D**. Using the same thread, stitch each bee body and head with cross

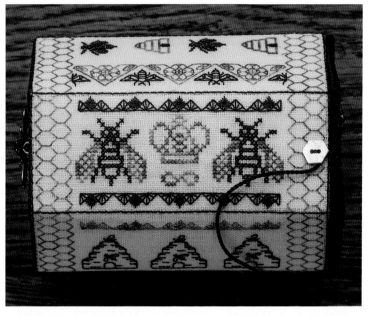

stitch over one thread and embroider the tip of the abdomen with a back stitch. Fill the gold border with diamond eyelets and half-diamond eyelets using **C**. Outline the serrated edge of the half-diamond eyelets with back stitch using the same thread.

Panels 2 and 5: Stitch the row of bees and skeps with cross stitch over one thread using **C** and **D**. Work the serrated floral design with double running stitch using **C** and the bees in the same manner using **D**.

Panel 3: Embroider the square and half-diamond eyelet borders in the same manner as panel 1 using **D**. Stitch the bees in cross stitch using **C** and **D** and the crown in the same manner using **C**.

Panel 6: Work the diamond and half-diamond eyelet borders in the same manner as panel 3. Stitch the project title in cross stitch over one thread using **C**. Choose the desired letters and numbers from the chart on page 163 and work the initials and date in cross stitch using the same thread.

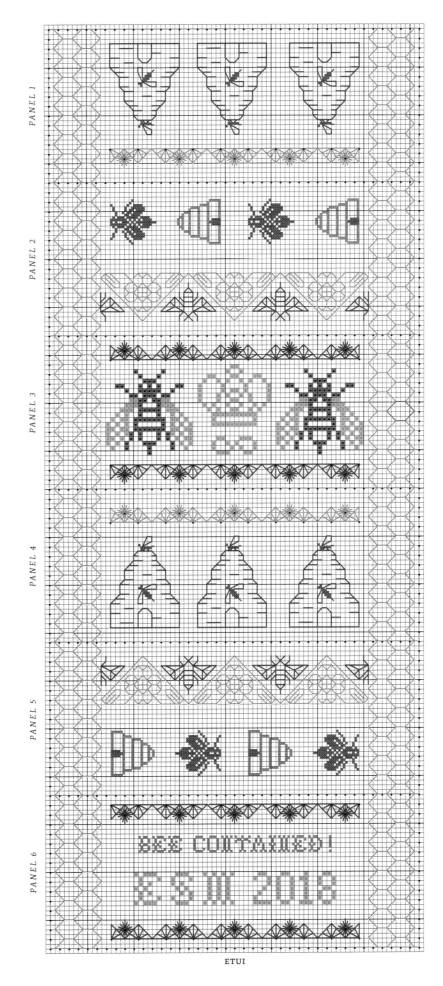

ETUI

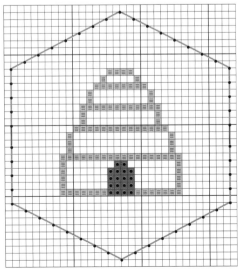

NEEDLEBOOK - *side 1*

NEEDLEBOOK

Side 1

Work the bee in cross stitch using **D** for the body, head, antennae and legs and **C** for the wings.

Side 2

Stitch the skep in cross stitch using **C** for the outline and bands and **D** for the opening.

SCISSOR FOB

Side 1

Using double running stitch or back stitch, work the floral diamond design with **C** and bees with **D**.

Side 2

Embroider the bee in cross stitch using **C**. Choose letters from the alphabet on page 163 and work the initials in the same manner using **D**.

PINCUSHION

All bands are worked using **C**. Stitch the first, third and sixth bands in long-arm cross stitch over six by four threads, the second and fifth bands in satin stitch and the fourth band in cross stitch over one thread. Work the opening in cross stitch using **D**.

RULER

Stitch the bee with cross stitch over one thread using **D** and the inch or centimetre markings with back stitch using the same thread. Embroider the numbers with cross stitch using **C**.

SCISSOR FOB - *side 1*

NEEDLEBOOK - *side 2*

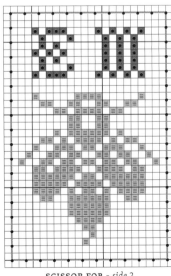

SCISSOR FOB - *side 2*

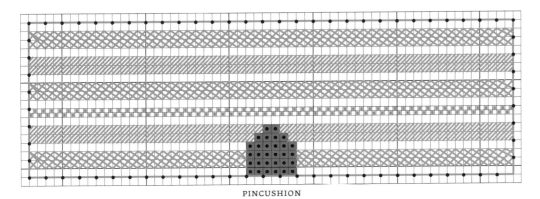

PINCUSHION

THREAD WINDER

Stitch the crown, bee bodies, heads, legs and antennae with cross stitch over one thread using **D** and the wings in the same manner using **C**.

construction

See pages 130 - 133.

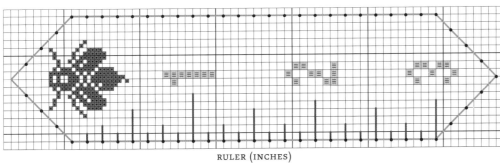

RULER (INCHES)

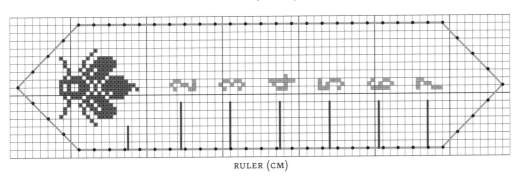

RULER (CM)

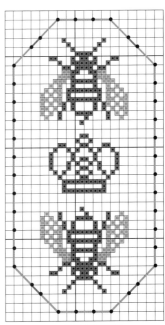

THREAD WINDER

gathering for winter etui

This design originated
from a desire to try a
new shape for an etui:
a cylinder with a lid that
was not simply a
flat top.

WHEN THINKING ABOUT THE THEME of the design, I decided on acorns because they are so often included in samplers, they are very popular and they symbolise strength and perseverance.

The box itself is covered in acorns in as many styles and stitches as I could come up with. If you look at the entire band, you'll see that it starts on the left with traditional images and becomes more stylised as it moves across the space. The pattern worked on the lid mimics the spiral pattern found on an acorn cap.

In the original construction I used cardboard, cylindrical, mailing tubes which were cut to size, but that requires a table saw, so there is an alternate method to constructing the box and lid using quilter's Mylar®.

I used a hand-turned wooden acorn for the end of the closure cord but you can certainly use any sort of charm or button.

before you begin

See pages 163 and 165 for the alphabet and number charts

We recommend that you read the complete article and construction information

All embroidery is worked with ONE strand of thread unless specified

this design uses

Back stitch

Brick stitch

Celtic cross stitch

Corded detached blanket stitch

Cross stitch

Diamond eyelet

Double running stitch

Four-sided stitch

French knot

Hedebo stitch loop

Queen stitch

Satin stitch

Smyrna cross stitch

Straight stitch

The finished etui measures 11cm x 7cm in diameter (4⅜" x 2¾").

requirements

Fabric

33cm x 64cm wide (13" x 25") light mocha 32-count linen

30cm x 60cm wide (12" x 23 ½") piece of copper silk dupion

Supplies

5cm x 50cm wide (2" x 20") strip of green wool felt

5cm x 7.5cm wide (2" x 3") piece of gold wool felt

20cm x 25cm wide (8" x 10") piece of lightweight fusible interfacing

7.5cm x 15cm wide (3" x 6") piece of medium weight fusible interfacing

23cm x 30cm wide (9" x 12") piece of interlining

10cm (4") square of thin wadding

23cm (9") square of Mylar® (polyester film)

11mm (⅜") hexagon mother-of-pearl button

3cm x 2.5cm wide (1⅛" x 1") wooden acorn

6mm (¼") amber faceted crystal beads (2)

Susan Clark Originals charm: C-1364 2cm x 15mm wide (¾" x ⅝") oak leaf

Contrasting sewing thread

Light orange beading thread

3cm x 2.5cm diameter (1¼" x 1") plastic or card cylinder*

Dressmaker's awl or large needle

Adhesive tape

Ruler

Craft knife

Craft glue

4.5cm x 6cm wide (1¾" x 2⅜") piece of firm card

Needles

No. 10 milliner's

No. 24 tapestry

No. 26 tapestry

Threads & Ribbon

DMC no. 12 perlé cotton

A = 842 vy lt beige-brown

Gloriana stranded silk

B = 115 topiary

C = 169 old gold

D = 193 copper

E = 206 olivine

F = 208 cocolat

G = 211 antique black

H = 213 thistle patch

I = 223 Havana brown

Gloriana 4mm silk ribbon

J = 113 autumn arbor – 90cm (1yd)

*Betsy used the plastic cylinder from the centre of a ball of perlé cotton

preparation for embroidery

PREPARING THE FABRIC

Neaten the edges of the linen with a machine zigzag or overlock stitch to prevent fraying.

TRANSFERRING THE DESIGN

Work all tacking lines along the grainlines using the contrasting thread. At the upper left-hand corner of the linen rectangle measure in and mark 5cm (2") from the upper and side edges. Beginning at this point and working over and under four threads, mark out each piece following the diagram (diag 1).

NOTE On each vertical side of the needle-book, long edges of the pincushion, and at the pointed end of the scissor sheath there are compensating stitches worked over two threads. Work under or over two threads at these points.

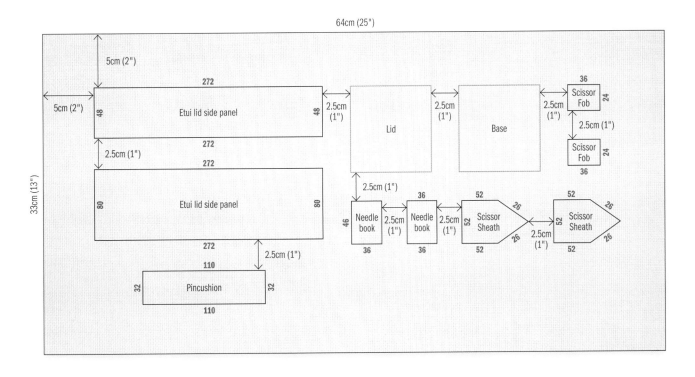

embroidery

Refer to the charts and close-up photographs for colour and stitch placement.

Use the no. 26 tapestry needle for all embroidery and the no. 10 milliner's needle and no. 24 tapestry for constructing the etui.

All embroidery is worked in the hand.

Each square on each graph represents 2 x 2 fabric threads.

ORDER OF WORK

All stitches are worked over two threads unless specified. On each panel work the back stitch outlines over four threads using **A**. Remove the tacking threads as you work.

The lid and base do not have an outline. On the needlebook, pincushion and scissor sheath, take care to work the compensating stitches over two threads.

HINT *When working cross stitch with variegated threads complete each cross before moving on to the next.*

ETUI

Lower side panel

Stitch the upper border with double running stitch or back stitch using **B**. Stitch the lower border in the same manner using **H**.

Acorn 1: Work the cupule with diamond eyelets over six threads alternating between **C** and **D**. Stitch the nut with brick stitch over four threads and the stalk with a back stitch using **E**.

Acorn 2: Embroider the motif with cross stitch over one thread using **F** for the stems, **E** for the leaf and **D** for the acorns.

Acorn 3: Work the inner shape with back stitch using **C** and the outer shape with four-sided stitch using **H**.

Acorn 4: Stitch the cupule and nut with double running stitch or back stitch using **I**, selecting a dark section of thread for the nut and a lighter section for the cupule.

Acorn 5: Embroider the cupule with Smyrna cross stitch using **D** and the nut with satin stitch using two strands of **E** and **F**. Stitch the stalk with cross stitch using **F**.

Acorn 6: Fill the cupule with corded detached blanket stitch using **I** and the nut with satin stitch using two strands of **C**.

Acorn 7: Stitch the stems, leaf and acorn outlines with double running stitch or back stitch using **G**. Fill the cupules with French knots using **F**, the nuts with satin stitch using **C** and the leaves with satin stitch using **C** and **E**.

ETUI - *lower side panel*

Colour Key   A   B   C   D   E   F   G   H   I

Acorn 8: Embroider the acorn with cross stitch over one thread using **B**.

Acorn 9: Work the cupule with queen stitch over four threads using **F** and the nut in the same manner using **D**. Stitch the stalk in back stitch using **F**.

Acorn 10: Outline the cupule and work the stalk with cross stitch using **E**. Fill the cupule with four-sided stitch using the same thread. Embroider the nut with cross stitch using **C**.

Acorn 11: Stitch the cupule with satin stitch using **G** and the nut in the same manner using **I**. Work the stalk with cross stitch using **E**.

Acorn 12: Work the stems, leaves and acorns with double running stitch or back stitch using **E**.

Acorn 13: Stitch the upper section of the cupule with four-sided stitch using **D**. Outline the band at the base with back stitch and fill with angled satin stitch using the same thread.

Embroider the nut outline with back stitch using **F** and fill with Smyrna cross stitch using the same thread.

Acorn 14: Fill the cupule with satin stitch using **H** then cover with a lattice of straight stitch using **G**. Work the stalk with cross stitch over one thread using **E** and the nut with satin stitch using two strands of the same thread.

Acorn 15: Stitch the cupule with Smyrna cross stitch variation alternating between **C** and **I**. Work the stalk with back stitch using **I**. Fill the nut with rows of satin stitch beginning at the upper edge with **F** and working through **E**, **D**, **I**, **F**, **E** to **D** at the base.

Acorn 16: Outline the cupule, nut, and work the stalk with cross stitch using **B**. Fill the cupule with the black work pattern with double running or back stitch using the same thread. Fill the nut with Smyrna cross stitch using **D**.

Acorn 17: Embroider the cupule with cross stitch over one thread using **B** and the stalk with cross stitch using **F**. Fill the nut with satin stitch using two strands of **E**.

Base

Stitch the squirrel and acorn with cross stitch using **I** for the squirrel, **C** and **F** for the acorn and **F** for the branch. Stitch the eye using **C**. Work the acorn motif on each side in the same manner as acorn 7. Choose the desired letters and numbers from the charts on pages 163 and 165 and work the date with cross stitch using **H** and the initials in the same manner using **D** and **E**.

Lid side panel

Work the acorn and leaf border at the base of the design with double running stitch or back stitch using **H**. Embroider the chequerboard design with cross stitch using **B**. Work a Smyrna cross stitch variation at the centre of each square using **C**, **D**, **E**, **F** and **I**. Outline the acorn with back stitch using **C** and fill the cupule with satin stitch and the nut with straight stitch using the same thread.

Lid top

Embroider the chequerboard design with cross stitch using **B**. Work a Smyrna cross stitch variation at the centre of each square using **C**, **D**, **E**, **F** and **I**. Work a diamond eyelet over fourteen threads at the centre of the lid using **A**.

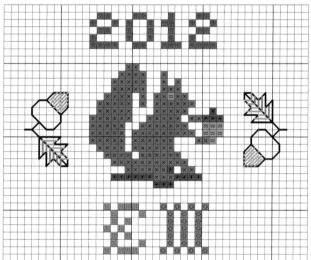

ETUI - *base*

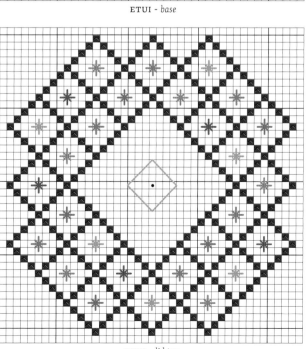

ETUI - *lid top*

ETUI - *lid side panel*

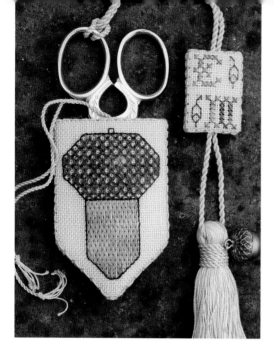

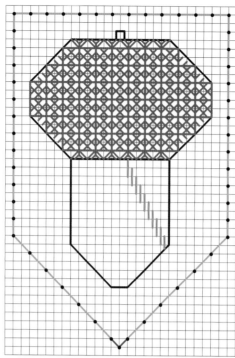

SCISSOR SHEATH - *side 1*

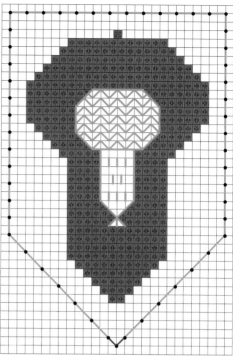

SCISSOR SHEATH - *side 2*

SCISSOR SHEATH

Side 1

Outline the cupule and nut and work the stalk in double running stitch or back stitch using **G**. Fill the cupule with Celtic cross stitch using **F**, working a half cross at the upper and lower edges, and the nut with brick stitch over four threads using **D**.

Side 2

Outline the centre motif with back stitch using **C**. Fill the cupule with double running stitch using the same thread. Work straight stitch over the nut and at the nut base using **C**. Fill the outer motif with cross stitch using **H**.

PINCUSHION

Stitch the trailing stem with cross stitch using **E**. Work the cupules with Smyrna cross stitch using **D** and fill the nuts with satin stitch using two strands of **C**.

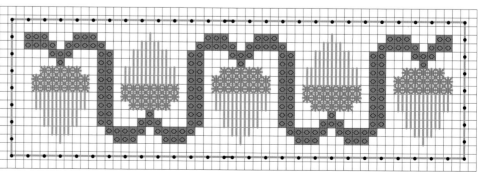

PINCUSHION

NEEDLEBOOK

Sides 1 and 2

Fill the oak leaf with cross stitch using **B**.

SCISSOR FOB

Side 1

Fill the cupule with Smyrna cross stitch using **I** and stitch the stalk with cross stitch using **F**. Fill the nut with satin stitch using two strands of **C** and **F**.

Side 2

Choose the desired letters from the chart on page 163 and work with cross stitch using **D** and **E**. Stitch the acorns with double running stitch or back stitch using **F**.

construction

See pages 134 - 137.

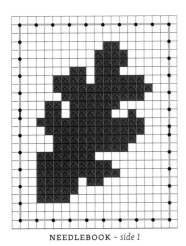

NEEDLEBOOK - *side 1*

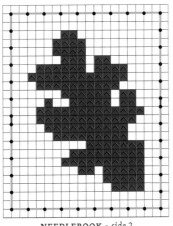

NEEDLEBOOK - *side 2*

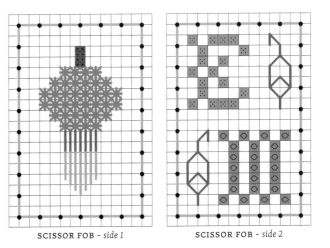

SCISSOR FOB - *side 1*   SCISSOR FOB - *side 2*

virgin queen's stitching pocket

The Virgin Queen's Pocket was originally designed for the 20th anniversary celebration of the Loudoun Sampler Guild in Virginia.

I TAUGHT THIS DESIGN ALL OVER THE US AND IN AUSTRALIA and each time I changed some of the motifs to reflect the area where it was being taught. The foxes have been replaced with kangaroos, pelicans, cardinals, armadillos, blue hens and bears. I also replaced the apples and apple blossoms with the state flower of each location.

This piece was designed shortly after the Virgin Queen's Stitching Wallet, taught at Beating Around the Bush, that was published in the first volume of *Willing Hands*. I consider it to be a companion to that design. They use the same colour palette and both include plenty of blackwork. Both were inspired by a scissor holder that was designed and stitched by one of my students, Laurie Doty of Livermore, California. Sadly, she passed away from cancer in 2016 just 2 weeks before she was due to attend the class that she inspired.

Of all of my designs the Virgin Queen wallet and pocket are my favourites. The name derives from the fact that they are in the style of Elizabethan band samplers and my home at the time was in Virginia, named for Elizabeth, the Virgin Queen.

this design uses

Algerian eyelet

Back stitch

Blanket stitch eyelet

Cross stitch

Double running stitch

Four-sided stitch

French knot

Hedebo stitch loop

Herringbone stitch

Long-arm cross stitch

Nun stitch

Queen stitch

Satin stitch

Square eyelet

before you begin

See page 163 for the alphabet and number chart

We recommend that you read the complete article and construction information

All embroidery is worked with ONE strand of thread

requirements

Fabric

15cm x 46cm wide (6" x 18") piece of ivory 32-count linen

12.5cm x 46cm wide (5" x 18") piece of willow silk dupion

Supplies

7.5cm x 30cm wide (3" x 12") piece of lightweight fusible interfacing

7.5cm x 25cm wide (3" x 10") piece of medium weight fusible interfacing

11.5cm x 28cm wide (4½" x 11") piece of interlining

Contrasting sewing thread

Green beading thread

Ruler

Craft knife

4.5cm x 6cm wide (1¾" x 2⅜") piece of firm card

Fine heat-soluble fabric marker

Needles

No. 10 milliner's

No. 24 tapestry

No. 26 tapestry

Threads & Beads

DMC no. 12 perlé cotton

A = 822 lt beige-grey

Gloriana stranded silk

B = 3 vanilla

C = 48 Spanish moss

D = 53 Granny Smith green

E = 106 desert rose

F = 151 cinnamon

G = 153 ollalieberry

H = 155 denim blue

I = 169 old gold

J = 217 canary

Miyuki no. 11 seed beads

K = 1003 silver-lined gold

AB (2)

The finished pocket measures 11.5cm x 7.5cm wide (4½" x 3") when closed and 24cm x 7.5cm wide (9½" x 3") when open.

preparation for embroidery

PREPARING THE FABRIC

Neaten the edges of the linen with a machine zigzag or overlock stitch to prevent fraying.

TRANSFERRING THE DESIGN

Work all tacking lines along the grainlines using the contrasting sewing thread. At the upper left-hand corner of the linen rectangle measure in and mark 4cm (1½") from the upper edge and 2.5cm (1") from the side edge. Beginning at this point and working over and under four threads, mark out each piece following the diagram (diag 1).

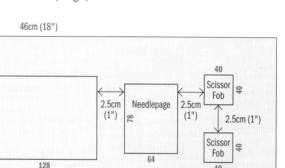

embroidery

Refer to the charts and close-up photographs for colour and stitch placement.

Use the no. 26 tapestry needle for all embroidery and the no. 10 milliner's needle and no. 24 tapestry for constructing the pocket.

All embroidery is worked in the hand.

Each square on each graph represents 2 x 2 fabric threads.

ORDER OF WORK

All stitches are worked over two threads unless specified.

On the pocket and fob panels only, work the back stitch lines over four threads using **A**. Remove the tacking threads as you work.

> **HINT** *When working cross stitch with variegated threads complete each cross before moving on to the next.*

POCKET

Front and base panels

Grapes

Using double running stitch or back stitch, work the grape foliage with **D**, the grapes with **G** and the border design with **H**. Embroider the yellow dividing band with long-arm cross stitch over four by two threads using **J**.

Apples

Work the apples in cross stitch using **F**, adding stitches over one thread where indicated to round the shapes. Outline each apple with back stitch using the same thread. Outline the flower petals with back stitch using **I** and fill with satin stitch using **B**. Fill the centre of the middle flower with five French knots using **J** and the centre of the side flowers with three French knots using the same thread. Work the stems and leaves with double running stitch or back stitch using **D**. Embroider the pink dividing band with long-arm cross stitch over four by two threads using **E**.

Colour Key

	A
	B
	C
	D
	E
	F
	G
	H
	I
	J

POCKET - *front panel & base*

Foxes

Work a cross stitch at the tip of each fox tail using **B**. Stitch the remainder of the panel with double running stitch or back stitch using **I** for the foxes, acorns and dividing line, and **F** and **G** for the flower.

Rose and lilies

Stitch the rose and rose hip motifs with double running stitch or back stitch using **C** for the rose stems and leaves, **D** for the rose sepals and rose hip stems and foliage, **E** for the petals and hips, and **J** for the rose centre.

Work the lily stems, foliage and flower outlines with double running stitch or back stitch using **G** and embroider the bud at the tip of each lily stem with queen stitch using the same thread. Fill the flowers with satin stitch using **J**.

Base

Choose the desired letters and numbers from the chart on page 163 and embroider with cross stitch over one thread using **D**, **F** and **H**.

Back panel

All embroidery is worked with **B**. Embroider bands 1 and 5 with satin stitch, bands 2 and 6 with four-sided stitch, and band 3 with four-sided stitch and Algerian eyelets. Embroider band 4 with satin stitch, the whole and half octagons with a complete and partial blanket stitch eyelets, and the diamonds with Algerian eyelets outlined with back stitch over four threads. Work band 7 with satin stitch and square eyelets over eight threads, and band 8 with herringbone stitch over six threads. Embroider the dividing bands with long-arm cross stitch over four by two threads.

8

7

6

5

4

3

2

1

POCKET - *back panel*

Needlepage

Stitch the diamonds with queen stitch using **I** and the remaining border with double running stitch or back stitch using **C** and **I**. Work the edging with nun stitch using **B**.

Scissor fob

Side 1

Embroider the foliage, petals and flower centre outline with double running stitch or back stitch using **D** and **G**. Work the sepals with queen stitch using **E** and the flower centre with cross stitch using **H**, working partial stitches where necessary.

Side 2

Choose two letters from the chart on page 163 and work in cross stitch using **F** and **J**. Embroider the flowers and border with double running stitch or back stitch using **B**, **C** and **D**.

construction

See pages 138 - 140.

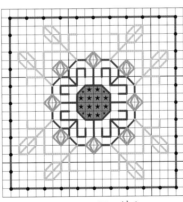

SCISSOR FOB - *side 1*

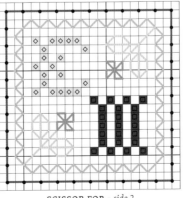

SCISSOR FOB - *side 2*

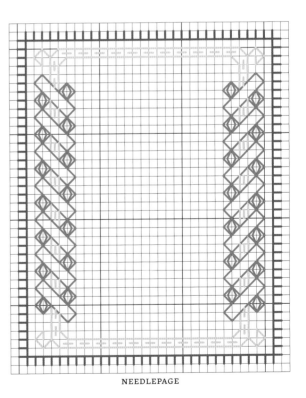

NEEDLEPAGE

bristol bag etui

The Bristol Bag was inspired by the samplers stitched by young girls at the George Muller orphanage in Bristol, England from the 1840s up until the early twentieth century.

THE VAST MAJORITY WERE WORKED IN RED THREAD on white linen, though there have been a rare few that were stitched in blue thread. The defining characteristics are multiple alphabets along with bands of patterns and, frequently, an image of a Bible. They are worked entirely in cross stitch.

For my stitching bag I chose one alphabet for the top of the bag and then took single motifs from the bands of patterns on the original samplers and scattered them over the bag.

Around this time, one of my students taught me how to do English paper piecing, a technique used in making quilts. It is very easy and I wanted to include it in a design. I found several red and white quilt fabrics that I used to make a pincushion and the base of the bag. The one difference between traditional paper piecing and mine is that in this project, the paper is left inside the fabric triangles to give them stability.

before you begin

See page 163 for the alphabet and number chart

We recommend that you read the complete article and construction information

All embroidery is worked with ONE strand of thread

this design uses

Back stitch

Cross stitch

Double running stitch

requirements

Fabric

33cm x 46cm wide (13" x 18") piece of antique white 32-count linen

28cm x 36cm wide (11" x 14") piece of red cotton

10cm x 23cm wide (4" x 9") piece of red and white print cotton

7.5cm x 38cm wide (3" x 15") piece of four different red and white print cottons

Supplies

7.5cm x 10cm wide (3" x 4") piece of red wool felt

25cm x 28cm wide (10" x 11") piece of lightweight fusible interfacing

28cm x 21.5cm wide (11" x 8½") sheet of comic board or firm card

90cm x 2cm wide (1yd x ¾") red and white chevron twill ribbon

6mm (¼") red button

Red sewing thread

Contrasting sewing thread

White beading thread

Fibre-fill

Paper piecing triangles: 1¼" – 16, 1½"- 8 or A4 sheet of firm paper

Ruler

Craft knife

Air-soluble fabric marker

Needles

No. 10 milliner's

No. 24 tapestry

No. 26 tapestry

Threads

DMC no. 12 perlé cotton

A = blanc

Gloriana stranded silk

B = 237 candy apple red

Gloriana 7mm silk ribbon

C = 237 candy apple red

The finished etui measures 16cm x 8cm wide (6¼" x 3⅛").

preparation for embroidery

PREPARING THE FABRIC

Neaten the edges of the linen with a machine zigzag or overlock stitch to prevent fraying.

TRANSFERRING THE DESIGN

Work all tacking lines along the grainlines using the contrasting thread. At the upper left-hand corner of the linen rectangle measure in and mark 2.5cm (1") from the upper edge and 4cm (1½") from the side edge. Beginning at this point and working over and under four threads, mark out each piece following the diagram (diag 1).

NOTE *On each edge of the scissor fob and the long edges of the thread winder panels there are compensating stitches over six threads. Work under or over six threads at these points. On the pointed ends of the thread winder panel, each short edge of the needlebook and on each side of each ribbon tab panel there are compensating stitches over two threads. Work under or over two threads at these points.*

embroidery

Refer to the charts and close-up photographs for colour and stitch placement.

Use the no. 26 tapestry needle for all embroidery and the no. 10 milliner's needle and no. 24 tapestry for constructing the etui.

All embroidery is worked in the hand.

Each square on each graph represents 2 x 2 fabric threads.

ORDER OF WORK

All stitches are worked over two threads unless specified. On each panel work the back stitch lines over four threads using **A**. Remove the tacking threads as you work. On each edge of the scissor fob and long edges of the thread winder panels take care to work the compensating stitches over six threads. On the pointed ends of the thread winder panel, short edges of the needlebook and on each side of each ribbon tab, work the compensating stitches over two threads.

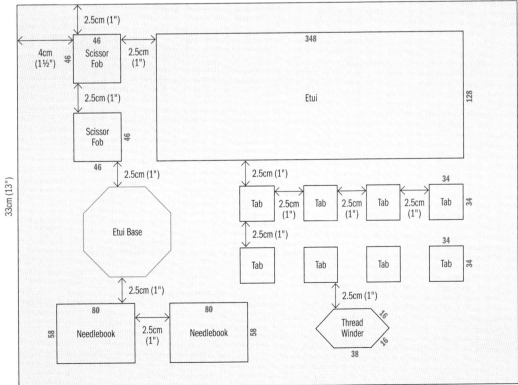

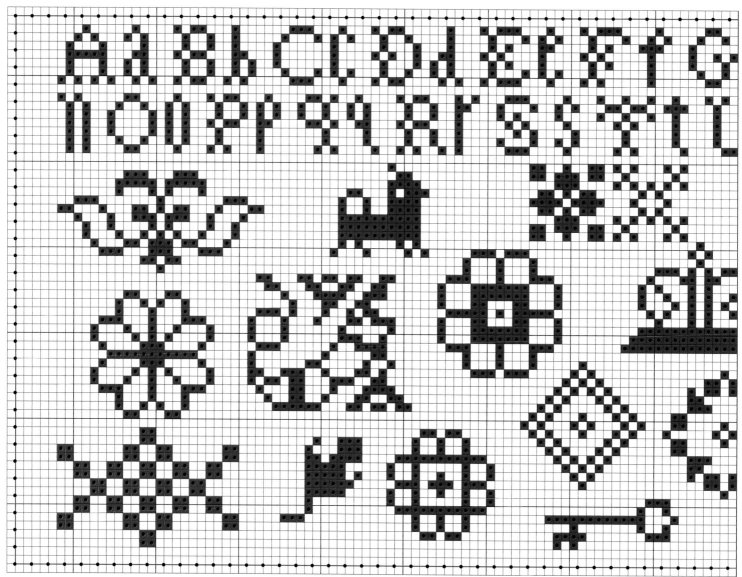

ETUI SIDE PANEL

ETUI SIDE PANEL

ETUI, THREAD WINDER AND SCISSOR FOB

Work the charted designs in cross stitch using **B**.

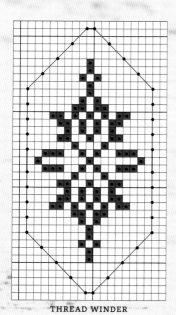

THREAD WINDER

ETUI BASE

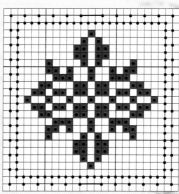

SCISSOR FOB - *side 1*

SCISSOR FOB - *side 2*

NEEDLEBOOK

Work the charted designs in cross stitch and double running stitch using **B**.

RIBBON TABS

Choose the desired letters and numbers from the chart on page 163 and work the initials, date and motifs in cross stitch using **B**.

construction

See pages 140 - 144.

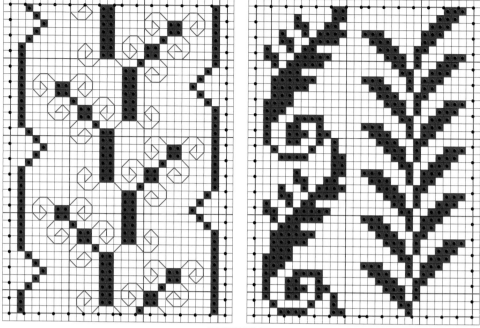

NEEDLEBOOK

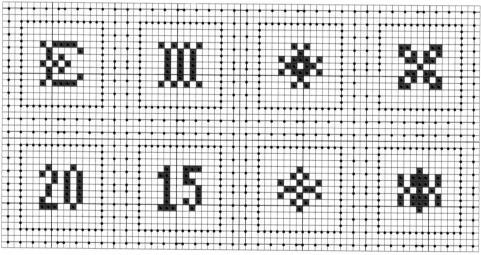

RIBBON TABS

exact change etui

Exact Change Etui was originally conceived as a "design your own" project.

I KNEW SO MANY WONDERFUL AND TALENTED NEEDLEWORKERS who had no confidence in their own abilities to form a design or to choose a colour palette and I wanted to nudge them into giving both a try.

When I taught this design, students had a choice of four colours of linen (magenta, blue, green and white) and I provided them with a colour palette that would work with any of the linen colours. I stitched my original on the magenta linen and provided the design charted as I stitched it. I also provided many pages of alternate bands and blocks that could be substituted as the stitcher desired. There is also a large variety of counted thread stitches and some may be new to even the most experienced stitcher. The differences produced by the classes were amazing!

For this book, the charts given are those matching my original model, but I encourage you to add or subtract thread colours and to change bands and blocks - this is a great opportunity to make a design that is truly your own!

before you begin

See pages 163–164 for the alphabet and number charts

We recommend that you read the complete article and construction information

All embroidery is worked with ONE strand of thread

this design uses

Back stitch

Celtic cross stitch

Cross stitch

Diamond eyelet

Double running stitch

Double woven cross stitch

Fly stitch

Four-sided stitch

Half-Rhodes stitch

Herringbone diamond stitch

Layered cross stitch

Long-arm cross stitch

Queen stitch

Rice stitch variation

Satin stitch

Smyrna cross stitch

Sprat's head stitch

Square eyelet

Straight stitch

Vandyke stitch

Waffle stitch

Woven stitch

The finished etui measures 13cm (5⅛") square.

requirements

Fabric

43cm (17") square of magenta 32-count linen

36cm x 28cm wide (14" x 11") piece of parrot green silk dupion

Supplies

5cm x 10cm wide (2" x 4") piece of green wool felt

25cm (10") square of lightweight fusible interfacing

25cm x 30cm wide (10" x 12") piece of medium weight fusible interfacing

23cm x 30cm wide (9" x 12") pieces of interlining (2)

4mm round jade bead

Dusky pink beading thread

Contrasting sewing thread

Fibre-fill

Ruler

Craft knife

Craft glue

4.5cm x 6cm wide (1¾" x 2⅜") piece of firm card

Needles

No. 10 milliner's

No. 24 tapestry

No. 26 tapestry

Threads & ribbon

DMC no. 12 perlé cotton

A = 224 vy lt shell pink

Gloriana stranded silk

B = 45 lacquered gold

C = 46 fallen leaves

D = 48 Spanish moss

E = 67 rain forest

F = 73 cottage woods

G = 81 hydrangea

H = 89 twilight

I = 96 summer foliage

J = 102 fresh snow

K = 124A slate blue light

L = 129 baby corn

M = 134 summer n smoke

N = 139 pomegranate

O = 142 Victorian garden

P = 156 Bordeaux

Q = 157 pumpkin

R = 179 iris

S = 180 tulip festival

Gloriana 7mm silk ribbon

T = 48 Spanish moss – 90cm (1yd)

preparation for embroidery

PREPARING THE FABRIC

Neaten the edges of the linen with a machine zigzag or overlock stitch to prevent fraying.

TRANSFERRING THE DESIGN

Work all tacking lines along the grainlines using the contrasting thread. At the upper left-hand corner of the linen measure and mark 4cm (1½") from the upper and side edges. Beginning at this point and working over and under four threads, mark out each piece following the diagram (diag 1).

embroidery

Refer to the charts and close-up photographs for colour placement.

Use the no. 26 tapestry needle for all embroidery and the no. 10 milliner's and no. 24 tapestry for constructing the etui.

All embroidery is worked in the hand.

Each square on each graph represents 2 x 2 fabric threads.

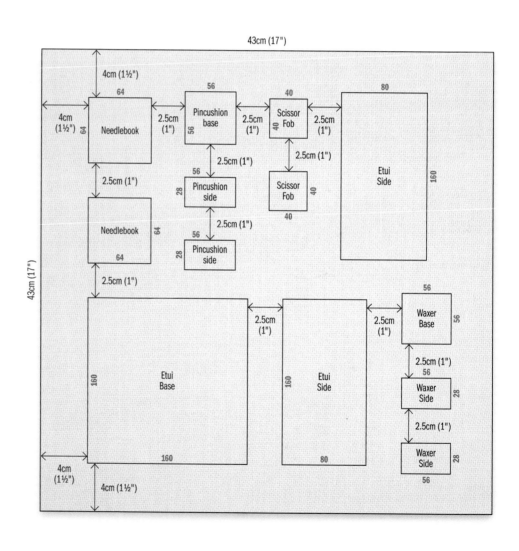

ORDER OF WORK

All stitches are worked over two threads unless specified.

> **HINT** *When working cross stitch with variegated threads complete each cross before moving on to the next.*

On the etui base and side panels, work Celtic cross stitch over four threads using **A** to form the borders, removing the tacking threads as you work. On each remaining panel work the back stitch lines over four threads using **A**. Remove the tacking threads as you work.

ETUI

Base

Outer border

Work the outer edges of the border at the top of the square with cross stitch using **M** and the centre section alternating layered cross stitch over four threads and double woven cross stitch over six threads using **L**. Work the small square at the left-hand side with sawtooth satin stitch using **N** and **Q** and the small square at the right-hand side with herringbone diamonds using **K** and **P**, alternating the colours. Work the centre motif and add cross stitch at the positions indicated using **K**. Stitch the border at the base of the square with double running stitch or back stitch using **I** for the foliage and **Q** for the flowers. Fill the small square at the left-hand side with alternating bands of Vandyke stitch over four threads using **K** and half-Rhodes stitch over six threads using **J**. Embroider the small square on the right-hand side with cross stitch over four threads, couched with a vertical straight stitch using **M** and upright cross stitch using **P**. Stitch the outer edges of the border on the left-hand side with cross stitch using **D** and **H** and the centre with two rows of sawtooth satin stitch using **B** and **S**. Work the border on the right-hand side with cross stitch using **D**, **N** and **R**.

Inner border

Work the top left-hand corner square in rice stitch variation over six threads using **R** for the cross stitch and **J** for the straight stitches. Fill the top right-hand corner square with woven stitch over three and two threads using **G** and **O**.

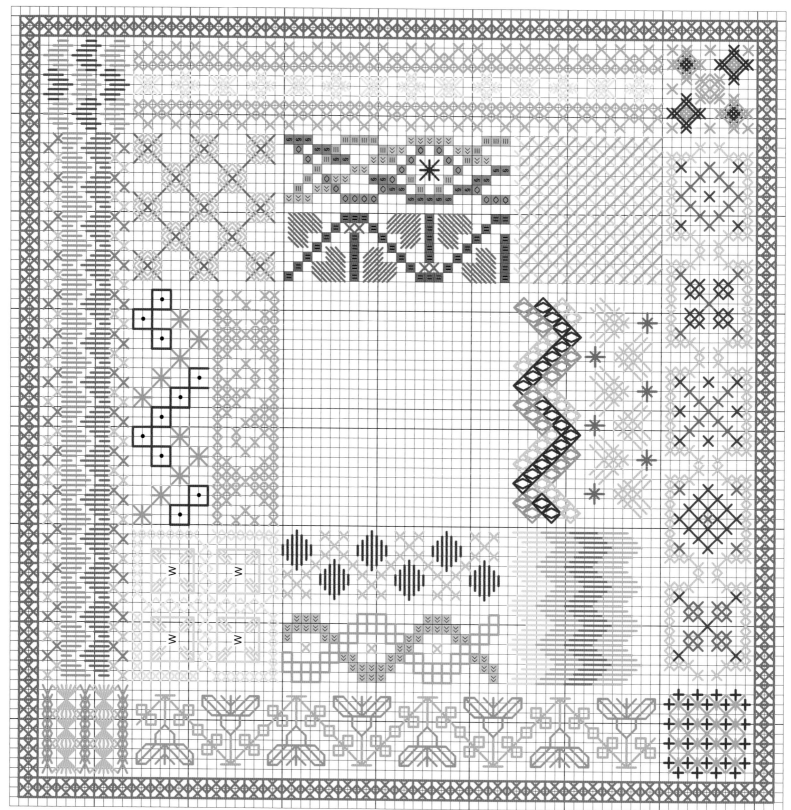

ETUI - *base*

Colour Key

☰☰☰		A	☰☰ ✳✳	K
☰☰ ✳✳	B	☰☰ ∈∈	L
☰☰ ■	C	☰☰ ⧄⧄	M
☰☰ ≪≪	D	☰☰ ▦	N
☰☰ ≡≡	E	☰☰ ⦂⦂	O
☰☰ ‡‡	F	☰☰ ◥	P
☰☰ ✳✳	G	☰☰ ○○	Q
☰☰ §§	H	☰☰ ⧄⧄	R
☰☰ ⦂⦂	I	☰☰ ‖‖	S
☰☰ ✧✧	J		

Stitch the intertwining lines in the upper half of the centre top border with cross stitch using **D**, **E**, **H** and **Q**. Embroider a Smyrna cross stitch at the position indicated using **P**. Work the lower half using **S** for the cross stitch lines and **R** for the satin stitch hearts.

Work the centre cross on the lower left-hand corner square with cross stitch over four threads using **L** and the remaining outline with cross stitch using the same thread. Fill each small square with waffle stitch over nine threads using **E**. Fill the lower right-hand corner square with four rows of sawtooth satin stitch using **E**, **I**, **K** and **S**. Stitch the upper half of the centre base border with cross stitch using **J** and satin stitch diamonds using **C**. Stitch the lower half using **D** and cross stitch for one intertwining line and **O** and four-sided stitch for the second line. Work a cross stitch at the centre of each lozenge shape using **J**.

Embroider the outer half of the left-hand side border with square eyelets over four threads using **P** and Smyrna cross stitch over four threads using **O**. Work the inner half in cross stitch using **M**.

Work the outer half of the right-hand side border with sprat's head stitch over ten threads using **J** and Smyrna cross stitch using **R**. Stitch the inner half with queen stitch over four threads using **D**, **P** and **Q**.

Choose letters from the alphabet on page 163 and work in cross stitch using **M**. If desired, work the year in cross stitch over one thread in the lower right-hand corner of the centre square using the same thread.

Side panels

Panel 1

This panel is divided into four sections and the instruction is written beginning at the top edge.

SECTION 1

Work the upper band with satin stitch over six threads using **O**. Stitch the lower band with back stitch and satin stitch using **H**. Embroider the small square at the right-hand end with cross stitch using **P**, square eyelets over four threads at the corners and a square eyelet over eight threads in the centre using **C**.

ETUI - *side panel 1*

SECTION 2

Stitch the upper band at the left-hand end with satin stitch using **D** and the lower band with cross stitch over one thread using **N**. Fill the centre block with satin stitch using **B**, **C**, **L**, **Q** and **P**. Work the floral band at the right-hand end with satin stitch and **J** for the flowers and double running stitch or back stitch using **O** for the foliage. Stitch the Greek key band with cross stitch over one thread using **G** and the remaining band with satin stitch using **S**.

SECTION 3

Using **M**, work the letters in cross stitch.

SECTION 4

Work the floral band with cross stitch using **I** and **L** for the flowers and **R** for the foliage. Stitch the Celtic knot at the left-hand end with back stitch using **J**.

Panel 2

This panel is divided into four sections and the instruction is written beginning at the top edge.

SECTION 1

Outline the upper and lower edges and part of the right-hand end of the long section with back stitch worked over four threads using **O**. Stitch each fan shape with straight stitch, radiating out from the same point using the same thread. Work a line of cross stitch over four threads and add a vertical stitch over the centre of the cross using **L**. Fill the small rectangle at the right-hand end of the band with Smyrna cross stitch using the same thread.

Fill the left-hand end of the lower band with cross stitch lines and satin stitch triangles using **G** and **P**. Embroider the right-hand end with sawtooth satin stitch using **D** and **Q**. Work a half-Rhodes stitch over seven threads between the two bands, adding two satin stitches over three threads at the centre using **J**.

SECTION 2

Work the square at the left-hand end with cross stitch for the corners and a diamond eyelet over fourteen threads at the centre using **M**. Stitch the upper band in two sections with double running stitch or back

stitch using **R** and work a half-Rhodes stitch at the centre in the same manner as section 1. Embroider the lower band in Smyrna cross stitch over four threads alternating **H** and **N**.

SECTION 3

Using **M**, work the letters in cross stitch.

SECTION 4

Work the floral band at the left-hand end with cross stitch using **B** and **L** for the flowers and **I** for the foliage. Stitch the chequerboard square with satin stitch using **J** and the heart band in the same manner using **K** for the hearts and **D** for the sawtooth edge. Embroider the four letters in the right-hand corner with cross stitch over one thread using **M**.

NEEDLEBOOK

Side 1

Work the design in cross stitch using **S**.

Side 2

Embroider the border in cross stitch using **D**. Choose the desired letters from the chart on page 164 and work in the same manner using **H**.

ETUI - side panel 2

NEEDLEBOOK - *side 1*

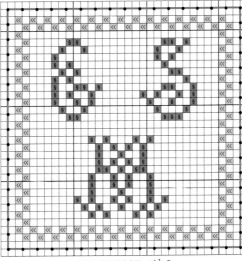

NEEDLEBOOK - *side 2*

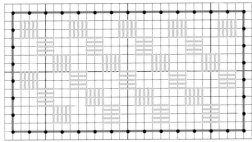

WAXER BOX - *side panel 1*

WAXER BOX - *side panel 2*

WAXER BOX - *base*

WAXER BOX

Base

Stitch the floral motifs with cross stitch using **I** for the foliage and **L** and **Q** for the flowers.

Side panels

Panel 1

Embroider the stepped blocks with satin stitch over four threads using **J**.

Panel 2

Work the floral border with cross stitch using **D** for the foliage and **H** and **N** for the flowers. Stitch the remaining border with Smyrna cross stitch over four threads, alternating stitches with **G** and **P**.

PINCUSHION

Base

Embroider the base with fly stitch over four threads using **O**.

Side Panels

Panel 1

Work the voided diamond border with cross stitch using **R**. Embroider the triangular motifs with satin stitch using **F**.

Panel 2

Stitch the floral motifs with cross stitch using **D** for the foliage and **G** for the flowers. Work the border of the remaining band with long-arm cross stitch over four by two threads using **K** and fill the centre with Smyrna cross stitch, alternating stitches over four and two threads using **P**.

SCISSOR FOB

Side 1

Embroider the border in cross stitch using **N**. Stitch the interlocking squares in the same manner using **G**.

Side 2

Choose the desired numbers from the chart on page 163 and work in cross stitch using **R**. Stitch the corner motifs in the same manner using **K**.

construction

See pages 145 - 147.

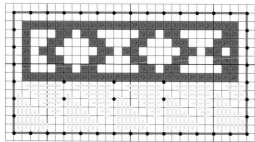

PINCUSHION - *side panel 1*

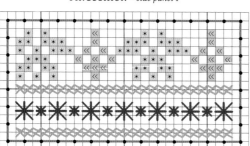

PINCUSHION - *side panel 2*

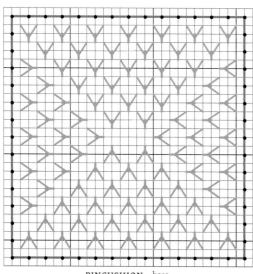

PINCUSHION - *base*

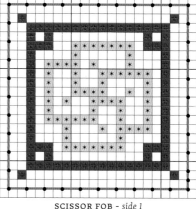

SCISSOR FOB - *side 1*

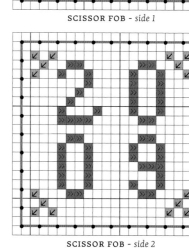

SCISSOR FOB - *side 2*

good for the goose box

Good for the Goose was inspired by the Canada geese that migrated through my area of Virginia.

WHEN WE LIVED ON OUR FARM, three of our neighbours had ponds on their properties that attracted the geese and we were inundated with them. They are pesky but also beautiful and I loved to see them flying in their V-shaped formations.

When thinking about what format this box would take, I went back to my years as a quilter for inspiration and settled on the "Geese in Flight" quilt pattern. It consists of triangles stacked one on top of the other so the box itself is triangular and most of the motifs are as well. I used a three-sided stitch on the borders because it mimics the quilt pattern. You'll notice that the triangles "fly" all the way around each panel.

I chose the linen colour because of its similarity to one of the feather colours of Canada Geese. The palette of threads was chosen because they are autumn colours and that is when the geese migrate.

before you begin

See page 164 for the alphabet chart

We recommend that you read the complete article and construction information

All embroidery is worked with ONE strand of thread

this design uses

Back stitch

Cross stitch

Double running stitch

Four-sided stitch

French knot

Hedebo stitch loop

Long-arm cross stitch

Satin stitch

Straight stitch

Three-sided stitch

Triangular Rhodes stitch

The finished box measures 13.5cm x 8cm wide (5⅜" x 3⅛").

requirements

Fabric

23cm x 46cm wide (9" x 18") piece of dark taupe 32-count linen

23cm x 46cm wide (9" x 18") piece of golden yellow silk dupion

Supplies

18cm x 38cm wide (7" x 15") piece of lightweight fusible interfacing

23cm x 28cm (9" x 11") pieces of interlining (2)

Golden yellow beading thread

Contrasting sewing thread

Ruler

Craft knife

Needles

No. 10 milliner's

No. 24 tapestry

No. 26 tapestry

Threads & Beads

DMC no. 12 perlé cotton

A = 822 lt beige-grey

Gloriana stranded silk

B = 01 charcoal

C = 10 winter woods

D = 48 Spanish moss

E = 51 slate green

F = 53 Granny Smith green

G = 102 fresh snow

H = 114 red clay

I = 131 sable

J = 138 Arctic ice

K = 169 old gold

12mm (½") triangular beads

L = carnelian (3)

Miyuki size 11 seed beads

M = 1003 silver-lined gold AB (45)

preparation for embroidery

PREPARING THE FABRIC

Neaten the edges of the linen with a machine zigzag or overlock stitch to prevent fraying.

TRANSFERRING THE DESIGN

Work all tacking lines along the grainlines using the contrasting sewing thread. At the upper left-hand corner of the linen measure and mark 5cm (2") down from the upper edge and 2.5cm (1") in from the side edge. Beginning at this point and working over and under four threads, mark out each piece following the diagram (diag 1).

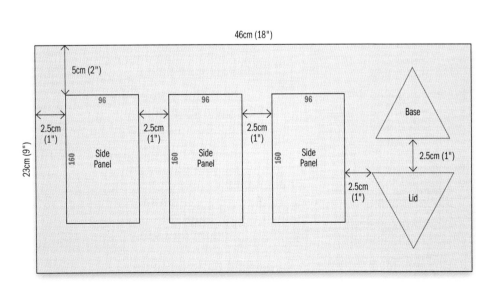

embroidery

Refer to the charts and close-up photographs for colour and stitch placement.

Use the no. 26 tapestry needle for all embroidery and the no. 10 milliner's needle and no. 24 tapestry for constructing the etui.

All embroidery is worked in the hand.

Each square on each graph represents 2 x 2 fabric threads.

ORDER OF WORK

All stitches are worked over two threads unless specified.

HINT *When working cross stitch with variegated threads complete each cross before moving on to the next.*

On the side panels, work three-sided stitch over four threads using **A** to form the borders, removing the tacking threads as you work and working a four-sided stitch at each corner.

SIDE PANELS

Each panel contains the same motifs but in a different order. The goose design varies on each panel but is stitched with the same colours.

Dividing lines

Work the heavy lines between each panel section with long-arm cross stitch over four by two threads using **B** and **I**.

Colour Key

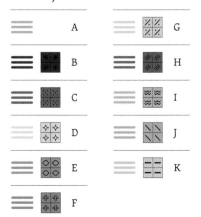

A		G		
B		H		
C		I		
D		J		
E		K		
F				

Eggs and grass

Stitch the eggs with cross stitch over one thread using **G** and each clump of grass with straight stitch, radiating from a single point, using **D**.

Goose outlines and grass

Embroider each goose with double running stitch or back stitch using **C**. Stitch a French knot for the eye using the same thread. Work each clump of grass with straight stitch radiating from a single point using **D**.

Bargello

All embroidery is worked with two strands.

Stitch the panel over four threads beginning at the upper edge with **K** and working through **J**, **G**, **H** and **D**. Embroider the half stitches at the upper and lower edges over two threads. Work the single black stitches over two threads using **B**.

Fir trees

Work the trees with satin stitch using **D** and **F**. Work a single straight stitch for the trunk on each one using the same colours.

Offset triangles

Embroider each triangle with satin stitch using two strands of **E**.

Intertwining lines

Stitch the intertwining lines with cross stitch using **D**, **H**, **J** and **K**.

Triangles

Work the triangles with half-Rhodes stitch, working one with each silk colour and two with one colour.

Goose

Embroider the goose in cross stitch using **B**, **G** and **I** for the body, tail, neck, head and legs, **C**, **H** and **I** where indicated for the wing and **K** for the eye. Where required, stitch the eggs with cross stitch over one thread using **G** and the grass with straight stitch using **D**. Stitch the borders with satin stitch over six and two threads using **A**.

LID PANEL

Embroider each goose with double running stitch or back stitch using **C**.

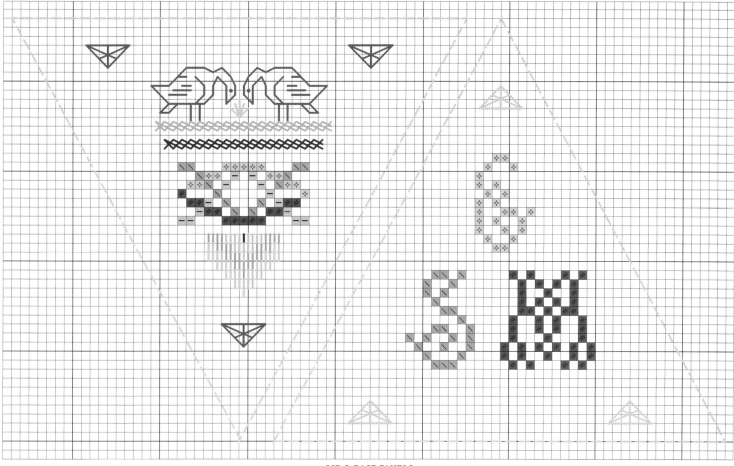

LID & BASE PANELS

Work a French knot for the eye using the same thread. Work the grass with straight stitch radiating from a single point using **D**. Embroider the heavy lines with long-arm cross stitch over four by two threads using **B** and **I**. Stitch the intertwining lines with cross stitch using **D**, **H**, **J** and **K**. Work the bargello with two strands, beginning at the upper edge with **K** and working through **J** and **G**. Add the single stitch at the upper edge with **B**.

Embroider a half-Rhodes stitch at each corner using **H**.

BASE PANEL

Choose the desired letters from the chart on page 164 and work with cross stitch using **D**, **H** and **J**. Work a half-Rhodes stitch in each corner using **G**.

construction

See pages 148 - 149.

cardinal pocket

The Cardinal Pocket was originally designed for the 5th anniversary celebration of the Winchester Chapter of the Embroiderer's Guild of America.

WINCHESTER, VIRGINIA, IS LOCATED in the Shenandoah Valley where apples are one of the largest crops and the cardinal is the state bird.

This is a small pocket etui that is meant to be worn as a necklace while stitching. It has a pocket for a small pair of scissors and a wool felt page for needles. It is worked in my two favorite counted thread techniques - blackwork and bargello. The bargello pattern is traditional and very old. The pull cord closure is the same as used on the Virgin Queen's Stitching Pocket.

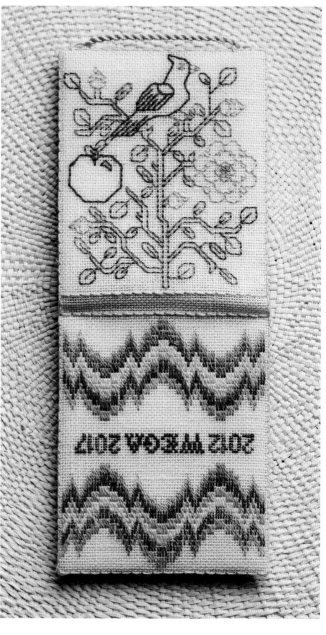

before you begin

See page 163 for the alphabet and number chart

We recommend that you read the complete article and construction information

All embroidery is worked with ONE strand of thread

this design uses

Back stitch

Cross stitch

Double running stitch

Hedebo stitch loop

Satin stitch

requirements

Fabric

20cm x 30cm wide (8" x 12") piece of cream 32-count linen

10cm x 45cm wide (4" x 17¾") piece of coordinating silk dupion

Supplies

5cm x 7.5cm wide (2" x 3") piece of gold wool felt

10cm x 23cm wide (4" x 9") piece of lightweight fusible interfacing

10cm x 18cm wide (4" x 7") piece of medium weight fusible interfacing

10cm x 23cm wide (4" x 9") piece of comic board or firm card

Cream beading thread

Contrasting sewing thread

6mm (¼") white buttons (2)

Ruler

Craft knife

4.5cm x 6cm wide (1¾" x 2⅜") piece of firm card

Fine heat-soluble fabric marker

Needles

No. 10 milliner's

No. 24 tapestry

No. 26 tapestry

Threads

DMC no. 12 perlé cotton

A = *822 lt beige-grey*

Gloriana stranded silk

B = *3 vanilla*

C = *53 Granny Smith green*

D = *141 sandstone rose*

E = *151 cinnamon*

F = *229 golden squash*

The finished pocket measures 7.5cm x 6.3cm wide (3" x 2½") when closed and 15.5cm x 6.3cm wide (6⅛" x 2½") when open.

preparation for embroidery

PREPARING THE FABRIC

Neaten the edges of the linen with a machine zigzag or overlock stitch to prevent fraying.

TRANSFERRING THE DESIGN

Work all tacking lines along the grainlines using the contrasting sewing thread.

At the upper left-hand corner of the linen rectangle measure in and mark 4cm (1½") from the upper and side edges. Beginning at this point and working over and under four threads, mark out each piece following the diagram (diag 1).

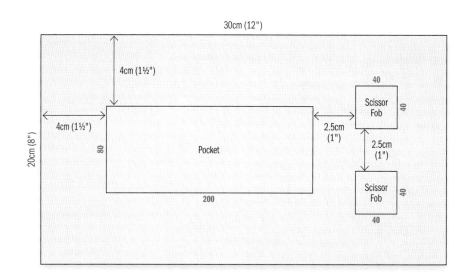

embroidery

Refer to the charts and close-up photographs for colour and stitch placement.

Use the no. 26 tapestry needle for all embroidery and the no. 10 milliner's needle and no. 24 tapestry for constructing the pocket.

All embroidery is worked in the hand.

Each square on each graph represents 2 x 2 fabric threads.

ORDER OF WORK

All stitches are worked over two threads unless specified.

On each panel work the back stitch lines over four threads using **A**. Remove the tacking threads as you work.

 HINT *When working cross stitch with variegated threads complete each cross before moving on to the next.*

POCKET

Front

Using **F** work the eye with back stitch and the flower centre with cross stitch. Embroider the remainder of the panel with double running stitch or back stitch using **C** for the stems and leaves, **D** for the flower petals and buds, **E** for the cardinal and apple, and **F** for the cardinal's beak and legs.

Back

Work the bargello with satin stitch over four threads. Stitch the upper band using **F**, **C**, **B**, **D**, **E** and **F**. Stitch the lower band as a mirror image of the upper band.

Choose the desired letters and numbers from the chart on page 163 and work in cross stitch over one thread using **C** and **E**.

SCISSOR FOB

Side 1

Embroider the apple with cross stitch using **E** and the stem, foliage and border with double running stitch or back stitch using **C**.

Side 2

Choose the desired letters from the chart on page 163 and work in cross stitch using **E** and **F**. Embroider the flowers and border with double running stitch or back stitch using **C** and **D**.

construction

See pages 150 - 152.

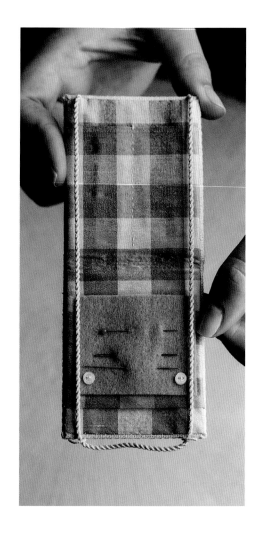

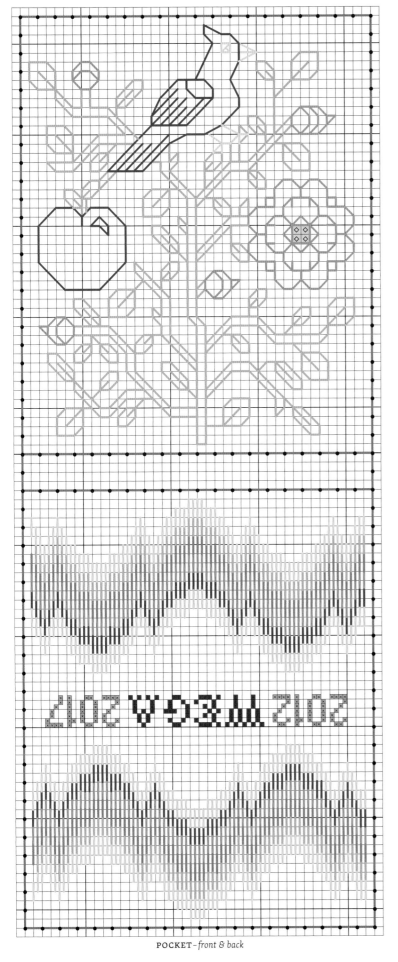

POCKET – *front & back*

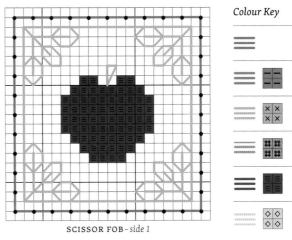

SCISSOR FOB – *side 1*

SCISSOR FOB – *side 2*

Colour Key

≡≡≡		A
≡≡≡	▦	B
≡≡≡	✕	C
≡≡≡	▦	D
≡≡≡	▪	E
∙∙∙	◇	F

mermaid bag etui

The Mermaid Bag was originally designed for a conference held by the Northwest Sampler Guild in Seattle, Washington. Their logo is stitched onto the first band of motifs.

ON THE CHARTS THIS LOGO has been replaced with a seagrass motif. The theme was inspired by a longtime stitching friend, Anne Cannizzaro, who we call the "queen of mermaids" since she adores them in any form.

The blue container that holds the bag is designed to be used for thread ends (orts). The mermaid inside the orts container is stitched over 2 x 2 linen ground threads, but she also appears on the scissor fob stitched over 1 x 1 linen ground threads.

The quotation on the bag itself is from William Shakespeare and the one on the orts container is from John Milton. The design originally included a couple of charms but over the years and throughout my teaching travels I have found and added many more. It is great fun to search and find them!

Rise, rise and heave thy rosie head from thy coral-pav'd bed.
John Milton

this design uses

Back stitch

Celtic cross stitch

Cross stitch

Diamond eyelet

Four-sided stitch

French knot

Long-arm cross stitch

Queen stitch

Satin stitch

Straight stitch

before you begin

See page 164 for the alphabet and number chart

We recommend that you read the complete article and construction information

All embroidery is worked with ONE strand of thread unless otherwise specified

The finished etui measures 13cm x 8.5cm wide (5⅛" x 3⅜").

requirements

Fabric

21cm x 46cm wide (8" x 18") piece of antique white 32-count linen

10cm x 25cm wide (4" x 10") piece of blue 32-count linen

25cm x 36cm wide (10" x 14") piece of blue and white sea-theme print cotton

12cm x 36cm wide (5" x 14") piece of blue and white wavy print cotton

Supplies

18cm x 33cm wide (7" x 13") piece of lightweight fusible interfacing

13cm x 33cm wide (5" x 13") piece of medium weight fusible interfacing

20cm x 25cm wide (8" x 10") piece of interlining

13mm (½") star-shape mother-of-pearl button

3mm (⅛") diameter seed pearl

Small pieces of coral with holes (12)

Mermaid charm

Assorted sea-theme charms (optional)

Susan Clark Originals buttons:
  BE-68 1cm (⅜") sand dollar button

  BE-162 12mm x 1cm wide (⁷⁄₁₆" x ⅜") scallop shell button

White sewing thread

Pale blue sewing thread

Dressmaker's awl or large needle

Ruler

Craft knife

4.5cm x 6cm wide (1¾" x 2⅜") piece of firm card

Needles

No. 10 milliner's

No. 24 tapestry

No. 26 tapestry

Threads

DMC no. 12 perlé cotton

A = blanc

B = 931 med antique blue

Gloriana stranded silk

C = 01 charcoal

D = 02 silver fox

E = 04 narcissus

F = 45 lacquered gold

G = 57 Pacific blue

H = 73A cottage woods lt

I = 88 seaweed

J = 89 twilight

K = 98 peach blush

L = 114 red clay

M = 116 olive grove

N = 119 dried pink roses

O = 131 sable

P = 133 pecan

Q = 134 summer n smoke

R = 138 Arctic ice

preparation for embroidery

PREPARING THE FABRICS

Neaten the edges of the linen with a machine zigzag or overlock stitch to prevent fraying.

TRANSFERRING THE DESIGN

Work all tacking lines along the grainlines using the contrasting thread. At the upper left-hand corner of the antique white linen rectangle measure in and mark 2cm (¾") from the upper and side edges. Beginning at this point and working over and under four threads, mark out each piece following the diagram (diag 1).

Mark out the orts pot design with tacking in the same manner, using the graph as a guide to completing the rectangle.

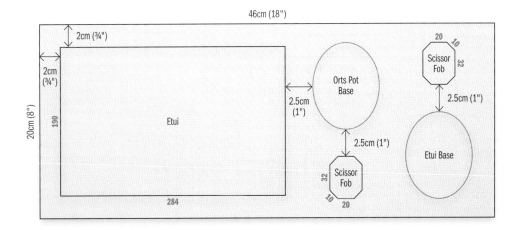

embroidery

Refer to the charts and close-up photographs for colour and stitch placement.

Use the no. 26 tapestry needle for all embroidery and the no. 10 milliner's needle and no. 24 tapestry for constructing the etui.

All embroidery is worked in the hand.

Each square on each graph represents 2 x 2 fabric threads.

ORDER OF WORK

All stitches are worked over two threads unless specified.

> **HINT** *When working cross stitch with variegated threads complete each cross before moving on to the next.*

On the etui panel, work Celtic cross stitch over four threads using **B** to form the lower and two upper borders, removing the tacking threads as you work. Do not remove the tacking marking the short edges. On the orts pot panel, work Celtic cross stitch over four threads using **B** along the lower and right-hand edges and back stitch over four threads along the upper long edge, removing the tacking along the stitched edges as you work. Do not remove the tacking along the remaining short edge. On the scissor fob panels work the back stitch lines over two threads using **B**. Remove the tacking threads as you work.

ETUI

Side panel

> **NOTE** *The rows of diamond eyelets are worked during construction.**

The instruction is written from the top edge down.

Work the band of small motifs beginning on the left-hand side:

MOTIF 1 – cross stitch over one thread using **C** and **O**.

MOTIF 2 – satin stitch using two strands of **G** and **J**.

MOTIF 3 – cross stitch over one thread using **I**.

MOTIF 4 – cross stitch over one thread using **O**.

MOTIF 5 – cross stitch over one thread using **C** and **O** and straight stitch using **E**.

MOTIF 6 – cross stitch over one thread using **N**, satin stitch using two strands of **J** and back stitch using **G**.

MOTIF 7 – cross stitch over one thread using **C**.

MOTIF 8 – satin stitch using **I**, **J** and **M**.

MOTIF 9 – straight stitch and back stitch using **N**.

MOTIF 10 – cross stitch over one thread using **L** and straight stitch using **F**.

MOTIF 11 – cross stitch over one thread using **C** and **P**.

MOTIF 12 – cross stitch over one thread using **E**.

MOTIF 13 – fanned straight stitch using **H** and **M**.

MOTIF 14 – back stitch and French knot using **I**.

MOTIF 15 – satin stitch using two strands of **D**, **G**, **H**, and **J**.

MOTIF 16 – cross stitch over one thread using **E** and **O**, back stitch using **O** and French knot using **E**.

MOTIF 17 – straight stitch using **J**, **K** and **N** and back stitch and straight stitch using **D**.

MOTIF 18 – cross stitch over one thread using **E** and **G** and straight stitch using **G**.

MOTIF 19 – queen stitch over four threads using **O** and back stitch using **C**.

MOTIF 20 – cross stitch over one thread using **C** and **Q** and straight stitch using **C**.

MOTIF 21 – cross stitch over one thread and straight stitch using **P**.

Embroider the solid band with long-arm cross stitch over six by four threads using **J**. Work the alphabet with cross stitch over one thread using **Q**. If desired, work your stylised initials with back stitch using **O**.

Stitch the four-sided stitch band over four threads using **I** and work a cross stitch at the centre of each square using **M**. Embroider the intertwining lines with cross stitch over one thread using **E**, **G**, **L** and **M**. Work the dashed-line border with satin stitch over two and four threads using **H**. Stitch the seagulls with cross stitch over one thread and straight stitch using **O**. Work the waves with satin stitch using two strands of **D**, **G**, and **R**.

Embroider the text with cross stitch over one thread using **R**. Work the starfish with cross stitch over one thread and straight stitch using **F**.

Base

Work the seaweed border with cross stitch over one thread and back stitch using **M**. Select the desired letters and numbers from the chart on page 164 and work the initials using **J**, **N** and **Q** and the date using **E** with cross stitch.

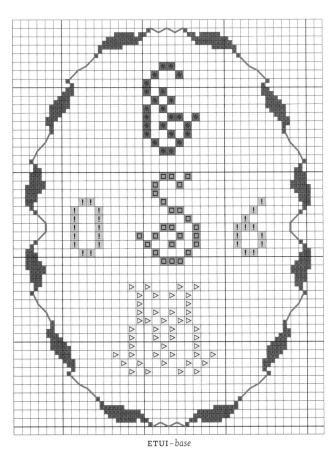

ETUI–*base*

Stars shot madly from their spheres to hear the sea-maid's music.

William Shakespeare

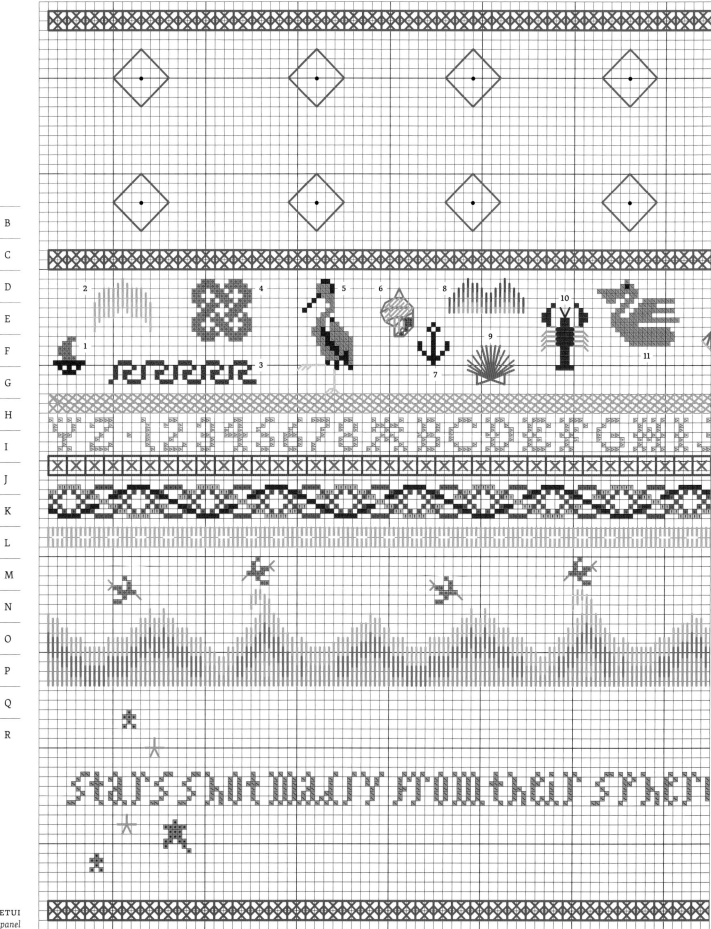

Colour Key

☰		B
☰	■	C
☰	⊡	D
☰	!!	E
☰	✳	F
☰	⊞	G
☰	◆	H
☰	▦	I
☰	☐☐	J
☰	‹‹	K
☰	■	L
☰	▤	M
☰	▨	N
☰	⊞	O
☰	✕	P
☰	▷▷	Q
☰	∿	R

ETUI
side panel

82

ETUI
side panel

ORTS POT – *base*

ORTS POT

Sides

Stitch the text with cross stitch over one thread using **O**.

Base

Work the mermaid with cross stitch and cross stitch over one thread using **F** for the hair, **K** for the arms, breasts and face outline, and **H** for the tail. Stitch the eyes with cross stitch over one thread and straight stitch using **G** and the nose and mouth in the same manner using **K**. Outline the upper shell

with back stitch and fill with straight stitch radiating from the base using two strands of **J**. Work the lower shell with back stitch using the same thread. Stitch the freshwater pearl at the marked position using **R**.

SCISSOR FOB

Side 1

Work the mermaid with cross stitch over one thread using **E** for the hair, **K** for the arms, breasts and face outline, and **H** for the tail. Stitch the eyes with straight stitch using **G** and the nose, mouth and chin in the same

manner using **K**. Work the tail markings with straight stitch using **H**. Outline the upper shell with back stitch and fill with straight stitch radiating from the base using **J**. Embroider the lower shell with back stitch using the same thread. Work the pearl with a French knot using **D**.

Side 2

Select the desired letters and numbers from the chart on page 164 and work the initials using **J**, **N** and **Q** and the date using **E** with cross stitch over one thread.

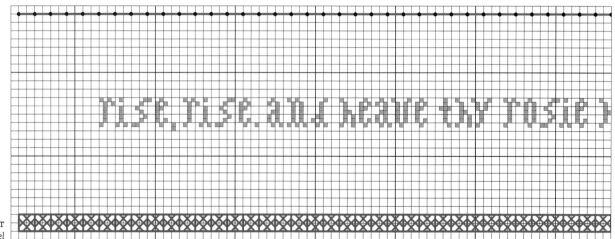

ORTS POT
side panel

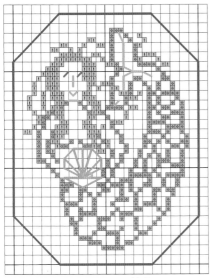

SCISSOR FOB–*side 1*

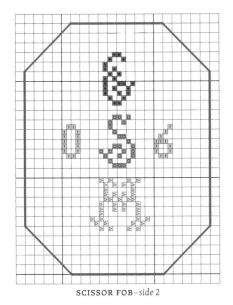

SCISSOR FOB–*side 2*

construction

See pages 152 - 155.

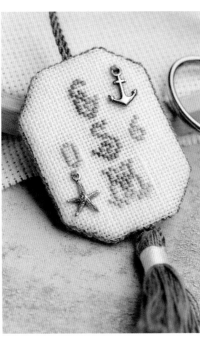

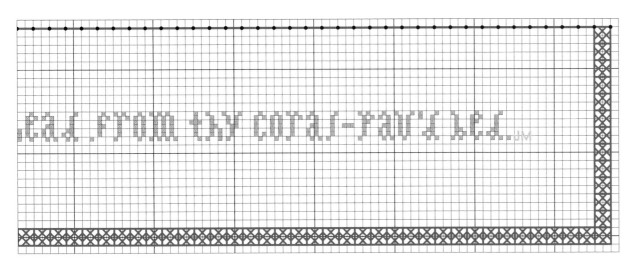

tasmanian needle tidy

The Tasmanian Needle Tidy resulted from a trip I made to that wonderful island after teaching at Beating Around the Bush in 2018.

I SPENT A FEW DAYS IN HOBART and was able to attend the Salamanca Saturday open market. Among the many treasures I saw was an old and very worn suede pocket tagged as a "needle tidy", a name that I had never heard before but instantly loved. When opened it contained wool needle pages and a small pocket with the words "odds and ends". I bought it, already seeing it as the format for a new design.

Some of the motifs on my design are based on my experiences and the things I saw while in Tasmania. Waves from a boat trip to Wineglass Bay, wallabies that I watched from my hotel room deck in Cole's Bay, and some of Tasmania's wonderful native flora. So many lovely memories!

this design uses

Algerian eyelet

Back stitch

Cross stitch

Double running stitch

Four-sided stitch

French knot

Long-arm cross stitch

Running stitch

Satin stitch

Spiral trellis stitch

Square eyelet

Straight stitch

before you begin

See page 163 for the alphabet and number chart

We recommend that you read the complete article and construction information

All embroidery is worked with ONE strand of thread

The finished tidy measures 11.5cm x 9.5cm wide (4½" x 3¾") when closed and 31.5cm x 9.5cm wide (12⅜" x 3¾") when open.

requirements

Fabric

18cm x 58cm wide (7" x 23")
piece of ivory 32-count linen

15cm x 51cm wide (6" x 20")
piece of antique violet silk
dupion

Supplies

8cm x 16cm wide (3⅛" x 6¼")
piece of violet wool felt

10cm x 46cm wide (4" x 18")
piece of lightweight fusible
interfacing

10cm x 41cm wide (4" x 16")
piece of medium weight fusible
interfacing

23cm x 28cm wide (9" x 11")
pieces of interlining (2)

Violet sewing thread

9mm (⅜") mother of pearl
button

Craft glue

Dressmaker's awl or large
needle

Ruler

Craft knife

Craft glue

3mm scallop pinking shears

4.5cm x 6cm wide (1¾" x 2⅜")
piece of firm card

Tracing paper

Fine black pen

Needles

No. 10 milliner's
No. 24 tapestry
No. 26 tapestry

Threads

DMC no. 12 perlé cotton
A = 3042 lt antique violet

Gloriana stranded silk
B = 80 bell flower
C = 89 twilight
D = 102 fresh snow
E = 130 sunflower
F = 180 tulip festival
G = 269 coral red light
H = 289 medium green
I = 295 Cotswold blue

preparation for embroidery

PREPARING THE FABRIC

Neaten the edges of the linen with a machine zigzag or overlock stitch to prevent fraying.

TRANSFERRING THE DESIGN

Work all tacking lines along the grainlines using the violet sewing thread. At the upper left-hand corner of the linen rectangle measure in and mark 4cm (1½") from the upper and side edges. Beginning at this point and working over and under four threads, mark out each piece following the diagram (diag 1).

NOTE *On the ends of the spine sections there are compensating stitches worked over two threads. On the upper and lower edges of the scissor fob there are compensating stitches worked over two threads. Work under or over two threads at these points.*

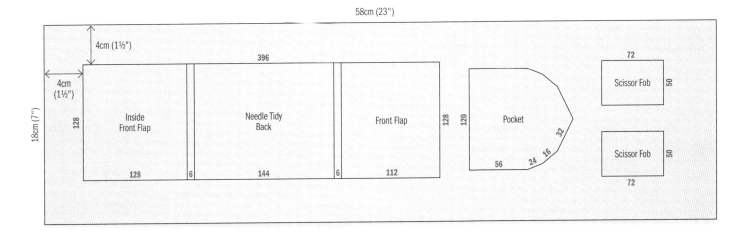

58cm (23")

4cm (1½")

4cm (1½")

18cm (7")

396

72

Inside Front Flap

Needle Tidy Back

Front Flap

Pocket

Scissor Fob

Scissor Fob

128

128

6

144

6

112

56

24

16

32

120

128

50

50

72

embroidery

Refer to the charts and close-up photographs for colour and stitch placement.

Use the no. 26 tapestry needle for all embroidery and the no.10 milliner's needle and no. 24 tapestry for constructing the needle tidy.

All embroidery is worked in the hand.

Each square on each graph represents 2 x 2 fabric threads.

ORDER OF WORK

All stitches are worked over two threads unless specified.

On each panel work the back stitch lines over four threads using **A**. Remove the tacking threads as you work. Take care to work the compensating stitches on the spine sections and scissor fob panels over two threads.

Referring to the chart and using **C**, embroider two square eyelets over six threads in the upper spine section, opening the eyelets so that a twisted cord can pass through them.

HINT *When working cross stitch with variegated threads complete each cross before moving on to the next.*

FRONT FLAP

Band A

Embroider the waves with cross stitch using **I**. Work the borders above and below the waves with long-arm cross stitch over four by two threads using **C**.

Band B

Using double running stitch or back stitch, work the wallabies with **B**, the centre flower with **G** and the buds and foliage with **I**. Fill the indicated area with four-sided stitch using **H** and work the border with running stitch using **G**.

Band C

Stitch the band with long-arm cross stitch over six by four threads using **F**.

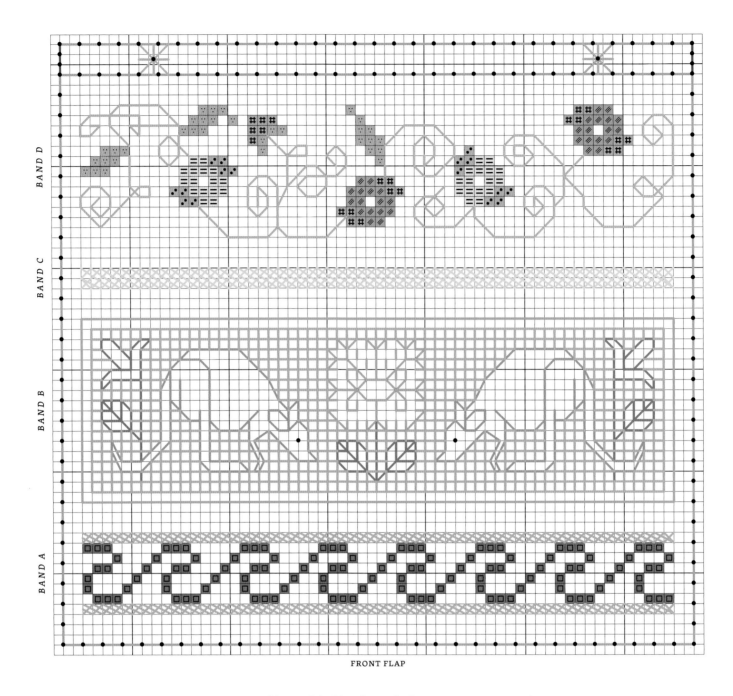

BAND D

BAND C

BAND B

BAND A

FRONT FLAP

Band D

Embroider the flowers and leaves with cross stitch using **B**, **C**, **E**, **G** and **H**. Stitch the stems and tendrils with double running stitch or back stitch using **H**.

BACK

Band E

Work the band with cross stitch and Algerian eyelets over four threads using **F**.

Band F

Using double running stitch or back stitch, embroider the twisted border with **I** and the

foliage of the blue flax and white gum with **H**. Stitch the blue flax flowers with spiral trellis stitch using **B**, and the gum blossoms with straight stitch over three or four threads and French knots using **D**.

Band G

Work the borders with sawtooth satin stitch using **C**. Embroider the snails with double running stitch or back stitch using **E**, **G** and **H**, working the tips of the feelers of the centre snails over one thread. Add a French knot eye to each centre snail using **E**.

Band H

Stitch the wattle with cross stitch using **E** and **H**.

INSIDE FRONT FLAP

Band I

Work the band of banksia flowers with double running stitch or back stitch, Algerian eyelets over four threads and four-sided stitch using **B**.

Band J

Embroider the centre line and diamonds with double running stitch using **C** and the remaining lines with cross stitch using **F**.

BAND H

BAND G

BAND F

BAND E

BACK

Colour Key   A   B   C   D

E   F   G   H   I

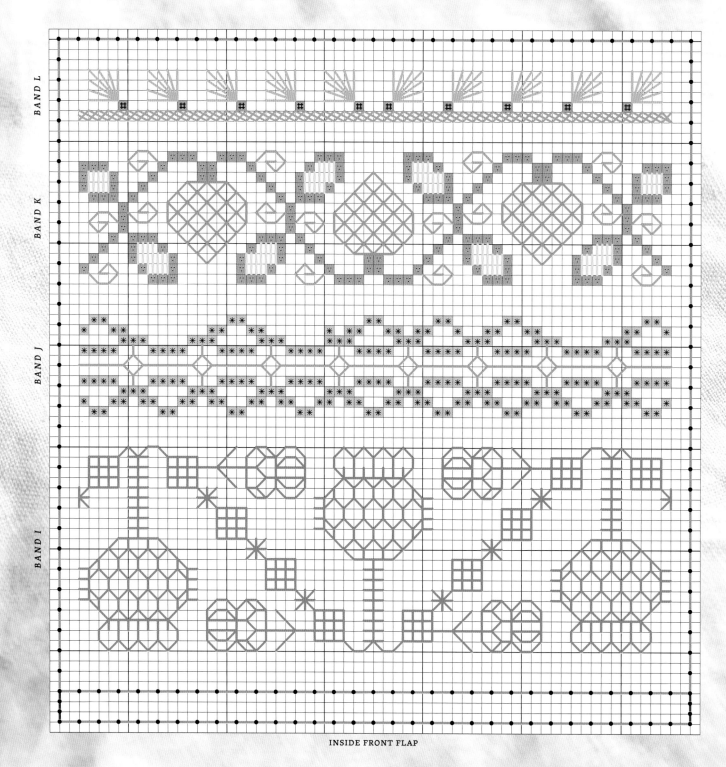

BAND L

BAND K

BAND J

BAND I

INSIDE FRONT FLAP

Band K

Work the strawberries and tendrils with double running stitch or back stitch using **G** and **H**. Stitch the stems and leaf outlines with cross stitch using **H** and fill the leaves with satin stitch using **E**.

Band L

Stitch the narrow band with long-arm cross stitch over four by two threads using **C** and the gum blossom stems with cross stitch using the same thread. Work each blossom with fanned straight stitches radiating from a single point using **D**.

POCKET

Stitch the border with double running stitch or back stitch using **E** and the lettering with cross stitch over one thread using **F**. Embroider the heart and leaves motif with cross stitch using **B**, **C**, **G** and **H**.

SCISSOR FOB
Side 1

Work the motif with cross stitch using **B**, **C**, **E** and **G** for the flower, **H** for the sepals and stem, and **I** for the leaves.

Side 2

Choose the desired letters and numbers from the chart on page 163 and embroider with cross stitch using **F** and **G** for the letters and numbers, **H** for the stems and **E** for the wattle flowers.

construction

See pages 156 - 158.

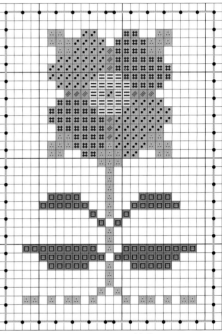

SCISSOR FOB – *side 1*

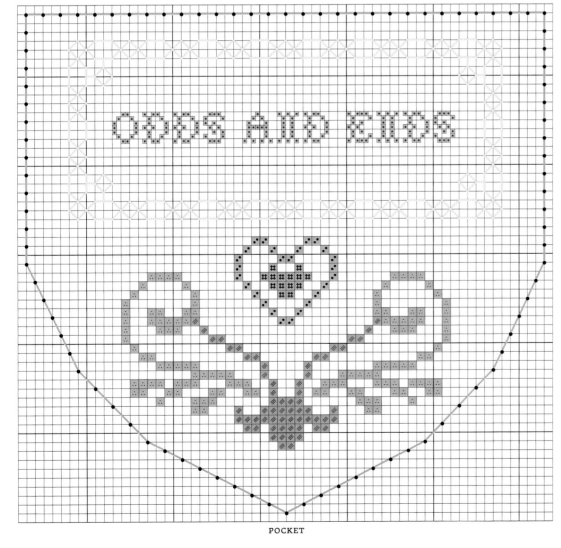

POCKET

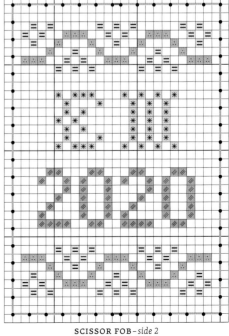

SCISSOR FOB – *side 2*

holbein hexagon etui

The Holbein Hexagon Etui is my last professional design as I retired at the end of 2020. Knowing that it would be the last one, I wanted to use my favorite counted thread technique - reversible blackwork, also known as Holbein stitch or double running stitch.

THE NAME OF THE STITCH comes from a painting of Jane Seymour that was done by Hans Holbein. In the painting blackwork can be seen on the outside of the jacket cuff on Jane's left wrist and on the inside of the cuff on her right wrist. The stitch was worked reversibly because it was used on clothing.

Reversible blackwork is my passion and I love it because I love puzzles. Reversible blackwork is certainly puzzling to many, but it can be mastered, like anything else in life, with practise. You may work this in back stitch if desired but it will look slightly different.

The format of the etui is based on an antique container that I saw at the Pioneer Memorial Museum in Salt Lake City, Utah. The container itself was made of six panels of some sort of heavy paper, laced together with cord. It was topped with an open style of netting that appeared to be stuffed with something, but I have no idea what is in it or what its purpose was. It did seem like a great way to add a pincushion to the lid of the box.

this design uses

Algerian eyelet

Back stitch

Double running stitch

before you begin

See page 165 for the alphabet
and number chart

We recommend that you
read the complete article and
construction information

All embroidery is worked with
ONE strand of thread

The finished etui measures
10cm x 9.5cm wide (4" x 3¾").

requirements

Fabric

43cm x 30cm wide (17" x 12") piece
of light mocha 32-count linen

50cm x 40cm wide (20" x 16") piece
of antique blue silk dupion

Supplies

5cm x 10cm wide (2" x 4") piece of
green wool felt

25cm (10") square of lightweight
fusible interfacing

10cm (4") square of medium weight
fusible interfacing

23cm x 28cm wide (9" x 11") piece
of interlining

28cm x 21.5cm wide (11 x 8 ½")
sheets of comic board or firm card
(2)

Ivory beading thread

Blue sewing thread

Fibre-fill

Ruler

Craft knife

4.5cm x 6cm wide (1¾" x 2⅜")
piece of firm card

Needles

No. 10 milliner's

No. 24 tapestry

No. 26 tapestry

Threads

DMC no. 12 perlé cotton

A = 842 vy lt beige-brown

B = 931 med antique blue

Gloriana stranded silk

C = 61 grape

D = 102 fresh snow

E = 134B summer gold

F = 155 denim blue

G = 201 hazelnut

H = 220 cinnabar

I = 277 iguana green

J = 304 auburn

K = 307 mesa sunset

Gloriana 4mm silk ribbon

L = 155 denim blue – 3.65m
(4yd")

preparation for embroidery

PREPARING THE FABRIC

Neaten the edges of the linen with a machine zigzag or overlock stitch to prevent fraying.

TRANSFERRING THE DESIGN

Work all tacking lines along the grainlines using the sewing thread. At the upper left-hand corner of the linen rectangle measure in and mark 2.5cm (1") from the upper and side edges. Beginning at this point and working over and under four threads, mark out each piece following the diagram (diag 1).

> **NOTE** *On each side of the needlebook and the upper and lower edges of the scissor sheath, there are compensating stitches worked over six threads. Work under or over six threads at these points.*

embroidery

Refer to the charts and close-up photographs for colour and stitch placement.

Use the no. 26 tapestry needle for all embroidery and the no. 10 milliner's needle and no. 24 tapestry for constructing the etui.

All embroidery is worked in the hand.

Each square on each graph represents 2 x 2 fabric threads.

ORDER OF WORK

All stitches are worked over two threads unless specified. On each panel, except the interior and exterior base hexagons, work the back stitch lines over four threads using **A**. Remove the tacking threads as you work. Use a looser tension for the back stitches on the vertical edges of the side panels. This will assist lacing the panels with ribbon. The hexagons are not outlined. On the needlebook and scissor sheath take care to work the compensating stitches over six threads.

> **HINT** *When working cross stitch with variegated threads complete each cross before moving on to the next.*

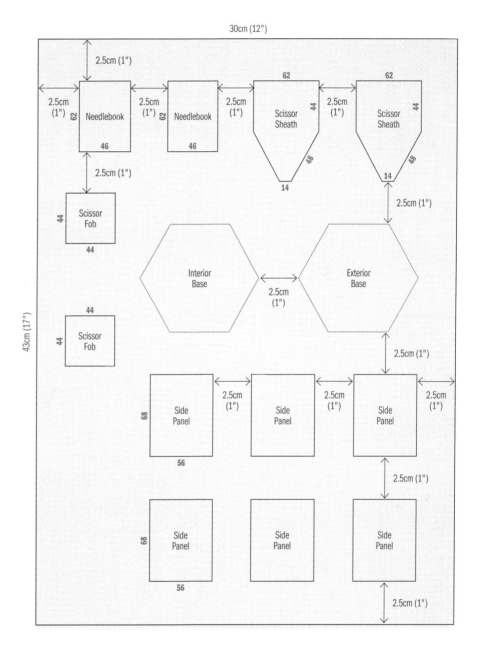

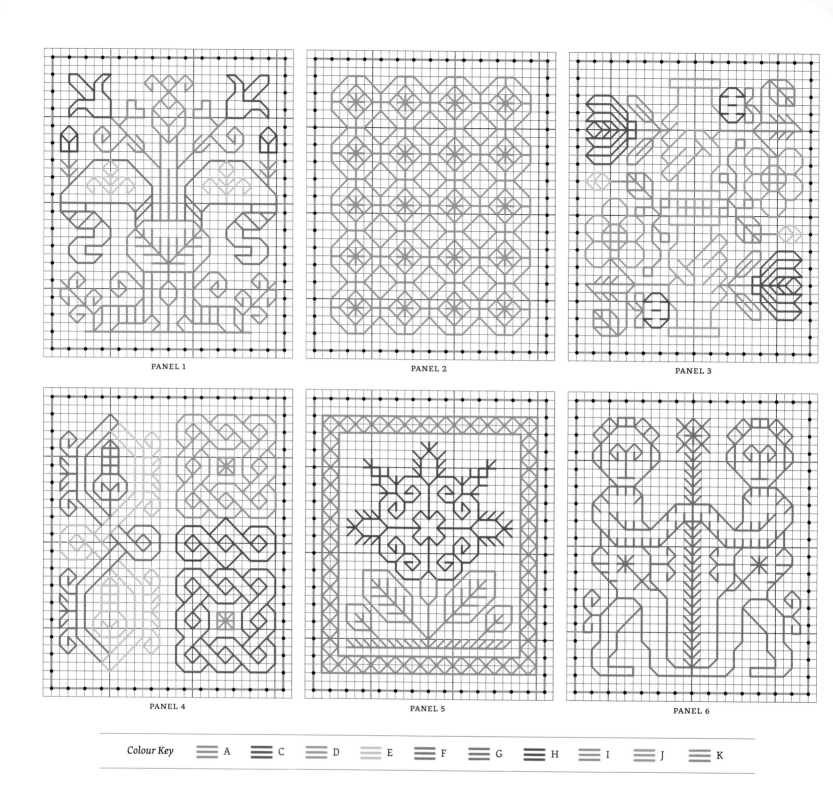

PANEL 1

PANEL 2

PANEL 3

PANEL 4

PANEL 5

PANEL 6

Colour Key   A   C   D   E   F   G   H   I   J   K

ETUI

All embroidery is worked using double running stitch or back stitch unless specified.

Side panels

Panel 1: Stitch the flowers using **C**, **E**, **F**, **H** and **J**. Work the vase and foliage using **I**.

Panel 2: Embroider the trellis and Algerian eyelets over four threads using **K**.

Panel 3: Stitch the hands using **D**, the flowers using **C**, **E**, **H** and **J**, and the foliage using **I**.

Panel 4: Work the left-hand motif with **E** and **F**, and the right-hand motifs with **C**, **H** and **J**. Stitch the Algerian eyelets over four threads and outlines using **D**.

Panel 5: Embroider the border with **K**, the flower with **H** and the foliage with **I**.

Panel 6: Stitch the figures and Algerian eyelets over four threads using **G**.

Interior base

Work the flowers using **C**, the foliage and Algerian eyelet over four threads using **I**, and the butterflies using **J**.

Exterior base

Choose the desired letters and numbers from the chart on page 165 and work the initials and date using **F** and **H**. Embroider the upper and lower borders using **K**, the flowers using **E** and the foliage using **I**.

INTERIOR BASE

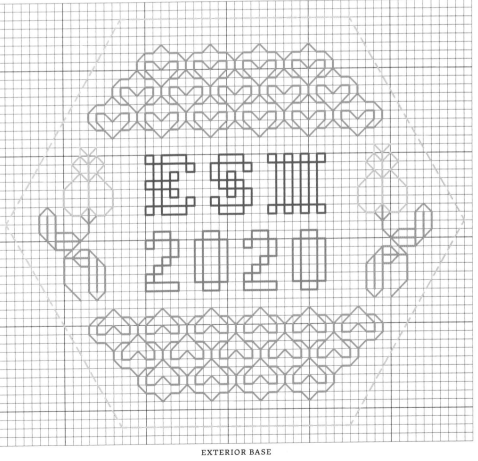

EXTERIOR BASE

NEEDLEBOOK – *side 1*

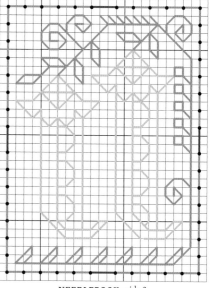

NEEDLEBOOK – *side 2*

SCISSOR FOB – *side 1*

SCISSOR FOB – *side 2*

NEEDLEBOOK

Side 1

Work the motif with **F**.

Side 2

Stitch the peas using **E** and the foliage using **I**.

SCISSOR FOB

Side 1

Work the acorns with **E** and the foliage with **G**.

Side 2

Embroider the pomegranate and bud using **H** and the foliage using **I**.

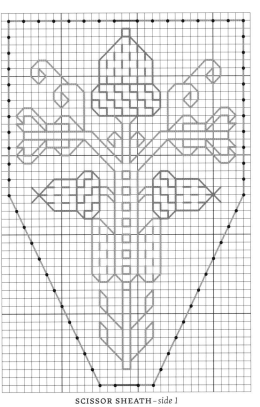

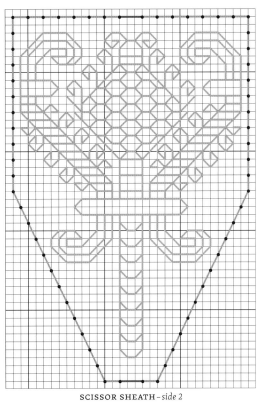

SCISSOR SHEATH – *side 1*

SCISSOR SHEATH – *side 2*

SCISSOR SHEATH

Side 1

Embroider the acorns using **G** and the foliage using **I**.

Side 2

Stitch the motif using **D**.

construction

See pages 159 - 162.

stitch guide

Algerian Eyelet

Working Algerian eyelets in a line is a different process than working them individually. Half of each stitch is worked in succession, then on the return journey the remainder of each eyelet is worked.

When working single eyelets, work each half before continuing on to the next.

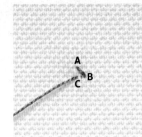

1 | Emerge at A, take the thread to the back at B and emerge at C.

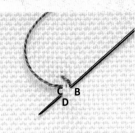

2 | Take the needle to the back at the centre (B) and emerge at D.

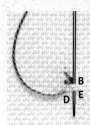

3 | Take the needle to the back at the centre (B) and emerge at E.

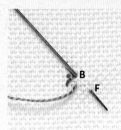

4 | Take the needle to the back at the centre (B) and emerge at F.

5 | Repeat steps 1–4. Continue in this manner for the required number of eyelets.

6 | Turn the work 180 degrees. Repeat steps 1–3 to complete the remaining half of the eyelet.

7 | Stitch the return journey in the same manner as step 6 to complete the diagonal row.

Binding a Tassel Neck

Tassels decorate various etuis and accessories in this book. The following method is used for binding each tassel, using a matching twisted cord. Refer to the construction information for making the twisted cords and tassels

1 | Leaving a short tail along the head of the tassel, loop the binding cord over the neck area as shown.

2 | Working from the top of the neck downwards, wrap the neck of the tassel for the desired length, leaving the upper end of the short tail and the loop uncovered.

3 | Take the wrapping cord through the loop, pulling it taut.

4 | Pull the short tail firmly upwards, closing the loop.

Continued next page...

**Binding a Tassel Neck /
continued**

5 | Continue to pull firmly so that the end of the loop is drawn up beneath the wraps.

6 | Trim each end of the binding cord as close to the wrapping as possible.

Blanket Stitch Eyelet

Blanket stitch creates a beaded edge around the eyelet. If desired, work a circle of running stitch at the position for the eyelet.

1 | With the emerging thread positioned at the lower edge, take the needle through the hole and outer edge of the eyelet, keeping the thread under the tip of the needle.

2 | Pull the thread through to create the first blanket stitch.

3 | Continue working blanket stitches in the same manner, turning the fabric as you work.

4 | When the edge is completely covered, take the needle to the back just over the loop of the last stitch.

5 | Pull the thread through. To secure, take the thread behind the blanket stitches on the wrong side.

6 | Completed eyelet.

Brick Stitch

Brick stitch adds texture as each row is offset to the previous row.

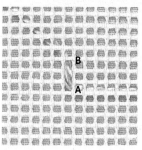

1 | Emerge at A and take the needle to the back at B. Pull the thread through.

2 | Emerge at C and take the needle to the back at D. Pull the thread through.

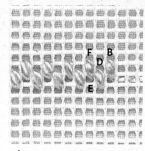

3 | Emerge at E and take the needle to the back at F. Pull the thread through. Continue working stitches across the row in the same manner.

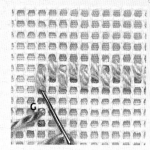

4 | Emerge at G and take the needle to the back through the same hole as the base of the previous stitch. Take care not to split the previous stitch.

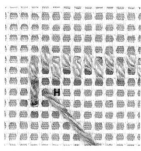

5 | Pull the thread through. Emerge at H.

6 | Take the needle to the back through the same hole as the base of the stitch directly above. Do not split the stitch.

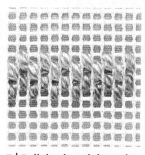

7 | Pull the thread through. Continue across the row in the same manner.

8 | Continue working rows of stitches back and forth in the same manner.

Celtic Cross Stitch

Also known as woven cross stitch, this can be used as a filling or as an ornate border. The second cross can be worked in a different colour if desired.

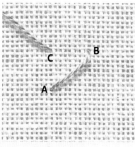

1 | Bring the thread to the front at A, take it to the back at B and emerge at C.

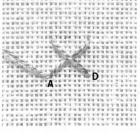

2 | Take the thread to the back at D and re-emerge at A.

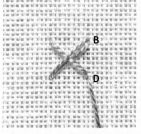

3 | Take the thread to the back at B and re-emerge at D.

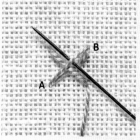

4 | Take the needle over the lower and under the upper threads between A and B.

Continued next page...

**Celtic Cross Stitch /
continued**

5 | Take the needle to the back at C.

6 | Pull the thread through.

Corded Detached Blanket Stitch

Detached stitches can be worked onto a cordonnet to create detached elements or a back stitch outline. Use a fine tapestry needle to avoid splitting the threads.

Here the stitch is shown worked onto a cordonnet.

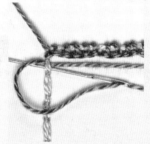

1 | Wrap the thread once around the left-hand side. Take the needle under the outline and work a detached blanket stitch over the upper edge.

2 | At the opposite side, slide the needle from right to left under the outline twice.

3 | Lay the thread across the shape and slide the needle under the outline from right to left twice on the opposite side.

4 | Take the needle behind the first purl of the previous row and the laid thread. Ensure the thread is under the tip of the needle.

5 | Take the needle behind the purl of the next stitch in the previous row and the laid thread, keeping the thread under the tip of the needle.

6 | Continue in this manner, working a detached blanket stitch into each purl of the previous row and over the laid thread.

7 | Wrap the thread twice around the outline on the right-hand side as before.

8 | Continue laying thread and working detached blanket stitch in this manner to fill the shape.

Diamond Eyelet

In counted work, eyelets are worked in a square or diamond shape. For each stitch, emerge at the outer edge of the eyelet and take the thread to the back through the centre.

1 | Emerge at A, on the outer edge of the eyelet, and take the thread to the back at the centre.

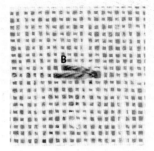

2 | Emerge at B, one fabric thread up and along from A, and take the thread to the back at the centre.

3 | Continue working in this manner and use a dressmaker's awl to help open up the eyelet as you work.

4 | Continue in the same manner around the eyelet, until every hole in the fabric around the outer edge of the shape has been used.

Double Running Stitch

Also known as Holbein stitch this is an effective way of creating a solid line of straight stitches that is the same on both sides.

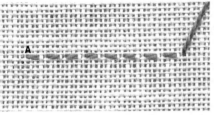

1 | Bring the thread to the surface at A. Work running stitch along the line over and under two threads.

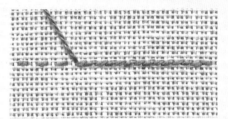

2 | Work a second line of running stitches in the remaining spaces to create a solid line of stitching.

Double Woven Cross Stitch

This stitch is formed by two rounds of overlapping diagonal straight stitches.

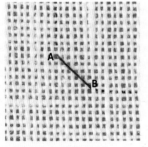

1 | First round. Work a stitch from A to B.

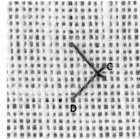

2 | Work a stitch from C to D, overlapping the end of the previous stitch.

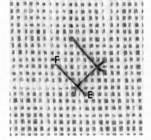

3 | Work the third stitch from E to F in the same manner.

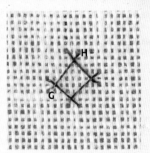

4 | Complete the first round from G to H, crossing over the first stitch.

Continued next page...

**Double Woven Cross
Stitch / continued**

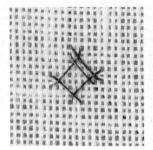

5 | Second round. Work a stitch to the inside of the first, one fabric thread towards the centre at each end, overlapping the previous stitches.

6 | Work a stitch one fabric thread in at each end from the second stitch, overlapping the previous stitches.

7 | Work a stitch along the third side of the round in the same manner.

8 | Complete the second round in the same manner, with the last stitch crossing over four previous stitches.

Four-sided Stitch

A regular pattern of thread squares is formed across the fabric.

1 | Take the thread from A to B.

2 | Take the thread from C to A.

3 | Take the thread from D to B.

4 | Take the thread from C to D.

5 | Continue the sequence to the end of the row.

6 | Continue to work squares across the subsequent rows working stitches as required. Turn the work 180 degrees after each row.

Half Rhodes Stitch

Half Rhodes stitch is Rhodes stitch worked to the halfway point, with straight stitches worked between one pair of opposite edges in a twist.

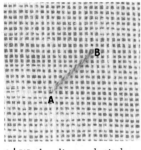

1 | Work a diagonal stitch from A to B, crossing the centre of the square from one side to the opposite side.

2 | Moving across one fabric thread, work a stitch from C to D, crossing over the first at the centre point.

3 | Continue moving across one fabric thread for subsequent stitches.

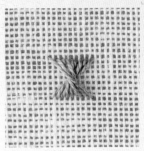

4 | The stitch is complete when every fabric hole along opposite sides of the square has been used once.

Hedebo Stitch Loop

The height of the loop is determined by the tension of the initial cross stitch. The looser the threads, the more height the loop will have.

1 | For the base of the loop, work a long cross stitch. Re-emerge at the left-hand side.

2 | Take the thread under the cross stitch from top to bottom, leaving a small loop.

3 | Take the needle through the loop, from back to front.

4 | Pull the thread through to tighten the knot, pulling the stitch to the left-hand end of the base threads.

5 | Repeat steps 2–4 to cover the base threads with Hedebo stitch. Ensure each stitch is pulled snugly against the previous to fill the loop.

6 | To finish, take the thread to the back at the right-hand side and secure.

Herringbone Diamond Stitch

This motif consists of a cross stitch surrounded by herringbone stitches worked in a clockwise direction. Each herringbone stitch begins one fabric thread away from the previous round. Change colour for the second and third rounds of stitching.

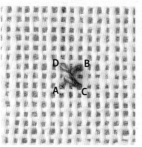

1 | Embroider a cross stitch over two fabric threads, A-B, C-D.

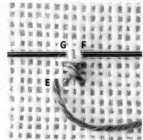

2 | Emerge at E, to the left of the cross stitch, and take the needle from F-G, above.

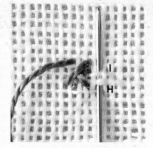

3 | Take the needle from H-I, to the right of the cross stitch.

4 | Take the needle from J-K, below the cross stitch.

5 | Pull the thread through and take it to the back at L, completing the first round.

6 | Emerging at M, repeat the sequence of stitching around the motif, one fabric thread away from the first round.

7 | Emerging at N, repeat the sequence one more time, one fabric thread away from the second round.

Herringbone Stitch

This stitch is often used to work decorative borders and fillings. Space the stitches closer or wider apart according to the desired effect.

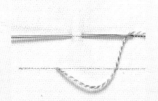

1 | Emerge on the lower line. With the thread below, take the needle from right to left on the upper line.

2 | With the thread above, take the needle from right to left on the lower line. Keep the stitch length the same as the previous stitch.

3 | With the thread below, take the needle from right to left on the upper line.

4 | Continue working evenly spaced stitches, alternating between the lower and upper lines.

5 | Closed herringbone stitch. Emerge in the same hole as the previous stitch.

Joining Stitch

Joining stitch is used to join panels neatly and evenly. Position the panels with edges and back stitches aligned.

 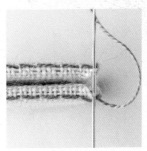  

1 | Emerge at the right-hand end on the lower panel.

2 | Take the needle under the linen thread on the opposite corner and the linen thread on the first corner, ensuring the fabric holes are aligned.

3 | Pull the thread through. Slip the needle back through the same hole on the lower panel and slide it behind the first back stitch.

4 | Pull the thread through. Take a stitch through the fold on each edge in the same manner as before, between the back stitches.

 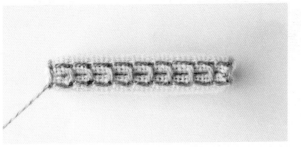

5 | Pull the thread through and slide the needle to the end of the next back stitch.

6 | Repeat steps 4 and 5 to the end of the row.

NOTE *To begin a thread, tie a knot in the end. Take the needle through the linen, and pull the thread firmly until the knot 'pops' through the fabric to the wrong side.*

To end a thread, tie a knot 6mm (¼") from the last stitch. Slide the needle back under the back stitches along the row just worked and emerge between two back stitches. Pull the thread through firmly until the knot 'pops' through the fabric. Maintaining tension on the thread, trim it close to the surface.

Layered Cross Stitch

This stitch, worked with overlapping cross stitches, creates a wide band that can be used for borders. A short line can be used as a spot motif. Each cross stitch is worked over four fabric threads and spaced one fabric thread from the previous stitch. The layered cross stitch on the Exact Change Etui is embroidered with three stitches.

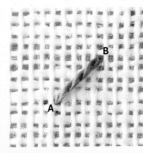 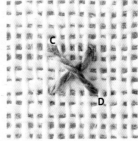 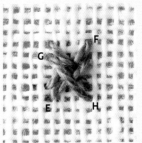 

1 | Begin a cross stitch, A-B.

2 | Take the thread behind the work horizontally to work the second stitch, C-D.

3 | Emerging at E, work a second cross stitch in the same manner, E-F, G-H.

4 | Work a third cross in the same manner to complete the row.

Long-arm Cross Stitch

Worked from left to right, this stitch forms a band with a plait-like texture.

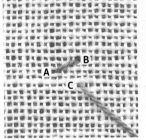

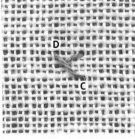

1 | Take the thread from A to B. This is half a long arm at the start of the row. Emerge at C.

2 | Take the thread from C to D.

3 | Work a long arm from E to F.

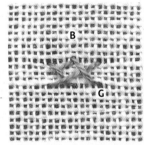

4 | Work a short arm from G to B.

5 | Continue along the row, working a long arm from left to right and a short arm from right to left.

6 | To end the row, work a half-length long arm.

Making a Twisted Cord

1 | Cut the required lengths of thread. Knot the threads together at each end.

2 | Hook one knotted end over a cup hook or sewing machine spool pin.

3 | Hook the second knotted end onto a spinster or cord drill. Alternatively, slide a pencil between the strands inside the knot.

4 | Keeping the threads taut, twist them until the twist has the desired tension.

5 | Keeping the threads taut, fold in half, bringing the knotted ends together.

6 | Working from the folded end, release the cord 5-10cm (2"-4") at a time until all the cord is twisted together. Add additional twist with your fingers.

7 | Remove the knotted end from the hook and knot the ends together.

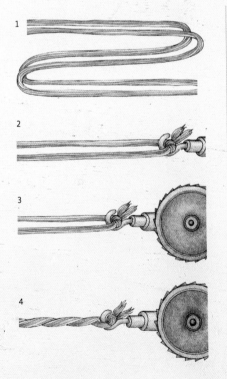

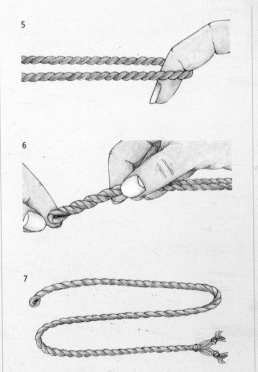

Two-colour Twisted Cord

This method creates a pretty cord where the colours are kept separate.

1 | Knot the ends of one colour together to form a loop. Pass the second colour through the loop and knot the ends together.

2 | Secure one knotted end over a hook or sewing machine spool pin.

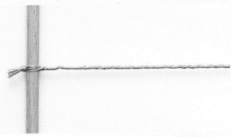

3 | Slide a pencil through the loop at the remaining end. Keeping the threads taut, turn until the threads are very tightly twisted.

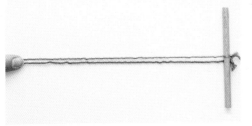

4 | Holding the point where the colours join, bring the knotted ends together and hold firmly, ensuring the tension is maintained.

5 | Working from the folded end, release the cord 5cm-10cm (2"-4") at a time..

6 | Continue to release short sections of the threads until the lengths are twisted together. Knot the ends together and trim away the previous knots.

Nun Stitch

This edging stitch is used where the excess fabric is to be cut away. The back stitches wrap the fabric threads and prevent the cut edge fraying.

Although each stitch is usually worked twice, here each one is worked once.

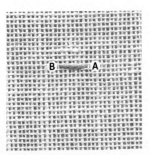

1 | Take the thread from A to B.

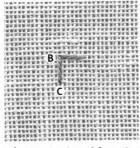

2 | Take the thread from C to B.

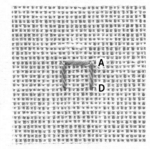

3 | Take the thread from D to A.

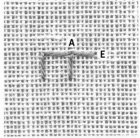

4 | Take the thread from E to A.

Continued next page...

**Nun Stitch /
continued**

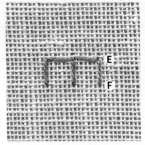

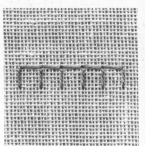

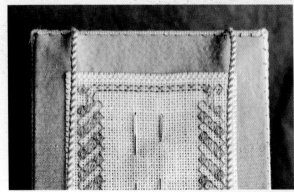

5 | Take the thread from F to E.

6 | Continue in the same manner to the end of the row.

Queen Stitch

This is also known as rococo stitch. Four laid stitches are couched in place, forming a tiny diamond. Each laid stitch shares the same hole at the upper and lower points, and each couching stitch is worked from left to right.

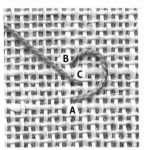

1 | Work a stitch from A to B leaving the stitch loose. Emerge at C, ensuring the thread is to the left of the stitch.

2 | Pull the thread through, tightening the first stitch.

3 | Take the thread to the back at D, one fabric thread to the right of C.

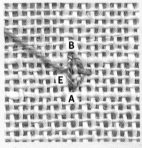

4 | Re-emerge at A. Take the thread to the back at B and emerge at E. The emerging thread is to the left of the stitch.

5 | Take the thread to the back at C.

6 | Re-emerge at A. Take the thread to the back at B and emerge at F.

7 | Take the thread to the back at E.

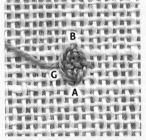

8 | Re-emerge at A. Take the thread to the back at B and emerge at G.

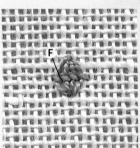

9 | Take the thread to the back at F to complete the stitch.

Rice Stitch Variation

Also known as raised knot stitch and square boss, rice stitch has the appearance of a cross worked through a circle. It can be used in a line or as an isolated stitch and can be worked in a single colour or a combination.

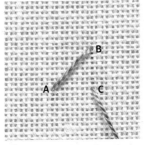

1 | Bring the thread to the front at A, take it to the back at B and emerge at C.

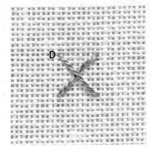

2 | Take the thread to the back at D.

3 | Bring the thread to the front at E. Take it to the back at F and emerge at G.

4 | Take the thread to the back at E and emerge at H.

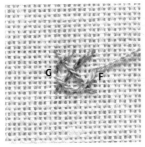

5 | Take the thread to the back at G and re-emerge at F.

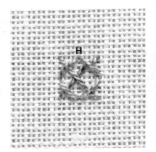

6 | Take the thread to the back at H and secure.

7 | Variation. Work three stitches over each arm of the cross stitch as shown, beginning with the outermost stitch for each group. The inner stitch is the same length as the outer.

Smyrna Cross Stitch

Smyrna cross stitch is formed from an upright cross stitch over a cross stitch.

1 | Work a stitch from A to B.

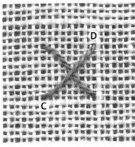

2 | Complete the cross stitch from C to D.

3 | Work a vertical stitch from E to F.

4 | Work a horizontal stitch from G to H.

Spiral Trellis Stitch

To create a higher dome, work more rounds of the spiral trellis before decreasing. The stitch can be worked in either a clockwise or counter-clockwise direction. The back stitch framework for the spiral trellis can be any shape; here it is octagonal.

1 | Framework. Outline the shape with back stitch over two threads. Emerge between the first and last stitches.

2 | Round 1. With the tip pointing outwards, slide the needle under the first stitch. Wrap the thread over and under the needle tip.

3 | Holding the wrap in place, pull the thread through to form a knot.

4 | Repeat steps 2–3 for each back stitch around the shape.

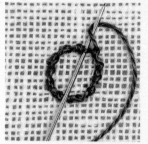

5 | Round 2. Slide the needle beneath the thread from round 1, just before the first knot. Wrap the needle tip as before.

6 | Pull the thread through.

7 | Work a stitch on the thread bar between each knot around the shape, continuing until the desired height is reached.

8 | Decrease. Work in a similar manner to step 7, skipping every second or third stitch until reaching the centre.

9 | Take the needle to the back over a thread bar across from the last stitch.

10 | Completed spiral trellis stitch.

Sprat's Head Stitch

This motif is made up of three pairs of overlapping stitches, creating the pointed shape named for the head of a fish. Here each stitch is worked over six fabric threads and the stitches at each side are aligned, one fabric thread apart.

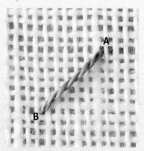

1 | Work a stitch from A to B.

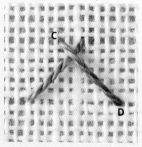

2 | Complete the pair with a stitch from C to D.

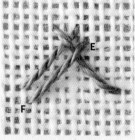

3 | Begin the second pair with a stitch from E to F.

4 | Complete the pair with a stitch from G to H.

5 | Work the third pair of stitches aligned with the previous stitches.

Square Eyelet

The outer edges of a square eyelet are aligned with the grain of the fabric. Move along one fabric thread for each stitch, always working from the outer edge of the square to the centre, pulling the stitches firmly to open the eyelet.

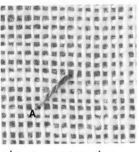

1 | Emerge at A, on the outer edge of the eyelet, and take the thread to the back at the centre.

2 | Emerge at B, one fabric thread along from A, and take the thread to the back at the centre.

3 | As you continue working the eyelet, maintain a firm tension and use a dressmaker's awl to help open the centre hole.

4 | Continue in the same manner around the eyelet, until every hole in the fabric around the outer edge of the square has been used.

Three-sided Stitch

This border stitch was designed to replicate the flying geese quilting pattern in stitch and is worked over four fabric threads.

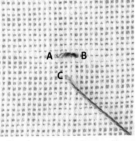

1 | Work a stitch from A to B and emerge at C.

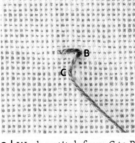

2 | Work a stitch from C to B and re-emerge at C.

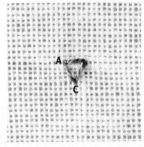

3 | Complete the triangle with a stitch from C to A.

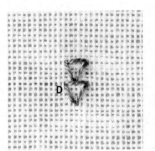

4 | Emerging at D, repeat the sequence to complete the second triangle.

5 | Repeat the sequence of three stitches to the end of the row.

6 | At a corner, work a four-sided stitch then continue with three-sided stitch.

Triangular Rhodes Stitch

Straight stitches are worked in a twist around the edges of a triangle. Here, the base of the triangle is worked over ten fabric threads.

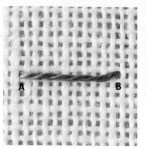

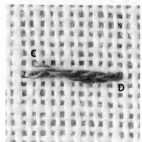

1 | Work the first stitch across the base of the triangle, A-B.

2 | Move along one fabric thread along the diagonal and base sides, C-D.

3 | Continue in the same manner to the apex of the triangle.

4 | Continue moving one fabric thread along the second diagonal side, ending just before the first stitch.

Vandyke Stitch

Short, wide cross stitches are worked over two by four threads in an overlapping manner to create a narrow band, with each stitch the same length.

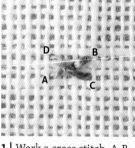

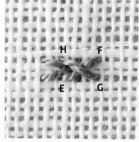

1 | Work a cross stitch, A-B, C-D.

2 | Beginning halfway along the previous stitch, work a second cross stitch E-F, G-H.

3 | Repeat step 2 to the end of the row.

Waffle Stitch

This stitch creates a distinctive, square motif with a woven texture and the appearance of a diamond within a square.
The square is always worked over an odd number of threads, with the initial cross stitch setting the size. Each stitch begins on the outer edge of the square in the lower half, and ends on the outer edge of the square in the upper half. Contrasting threads have been used for clarity.
In each step, the stitch being worked is shown in brown.

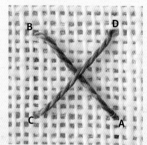

1 | Begin with a large cross stitch over nine threads, A-B, C-D.

2 | Work a pair of stitches to cross in the upper half of the square, E-F, G-H.

3 | Work the next pair of stitches to cross in the lower half of the square, I-J, K-L.

4 | Work an upper pair, beginning each stitch at M and N.

5 | Stitch a lower pair, beginning at O and P.

6 | Stitch an upper pair, beginning at Q and R.

7 | Work a lower pair, beginning at S and T.

8 | Complete the upper half with stitches beginning at U and V.

9 | Complete the lower half with stitches beginning at W and X.

Woven Stitch

This stitch uses two threads worked in an overlapping manner to create a woven pattern, and each diagonal stitch is worked over three fabric threads. Use two needles, one for each thread.

1 | First thread: Work a row of diagonal stitches from left to right.

2 | Second thread: Work diagonal stitches from right to left, offsetting them to the previous row by one horizontal fabric thread.

3 | First thread: Work a stitch from A to B, three fabric threads below the first row.

4 | Continue in the same manner to the end of the row, working from right to left.

5 | Second thread: Work a stitch from C to D, three fabric threads below the second row.

6 | Continue in the same manner to the end of the row, working from left to right.

7 | Repeat steps 1-6 as needed to fill the required area.

basic stitches

Back Stitch

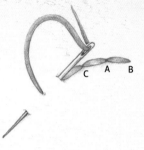

C A B

Cross Stitch

Fly Stitch

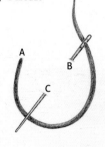

A

B

C

D

French Knot

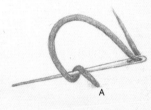

A

B A

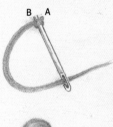

Running Stitch

Satin Stitch

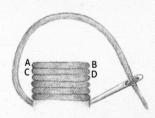

A B
C D

Straight Stitch

kits

Inspirations
Ready-to-Stitch kits
are available at
inspirationsstudios.com

bee contained etui

Page 8

Kit contains: Fabrics, interfacing, interlining, comic board, wool felt, buttons, charms, beading thread, embroidery threads, ribbon and needles

gathering for winter etui

Page 18

Kit contains: Fabrics, interfacings, interlining, wadding, wool felts, Mylar®, button, wooden acorn, charm, beading thread, embroidery threads, beads, ribbon and needles

virgin queen's stitching pocket

Page 30

Kit contains: Fabrics, interfacings, interlining, beading thread, embroidery threads, beads and needles

bristol bag etui

Page 38

Kit contains: Fabrics, interfacing, comic board, firm paper, wool felt, button, red sewing thread, beading thread, embroidery threads, ribbons and needles

exact change etui

Page 48

Kit contains: Fabrics, interfacings, interlining, wool felt, beading thread, embroidery threads, bead and needles

good for the goose box

Page 60

Kit contains: Fabrics, interfacing, interlining, beading thread, embroidery threads, beads and needles

cardinal pocket

Page 70

Kit contains: Fabrics, interfacings, comic board, wool felt, buttons, beading thread, embroidery threads, and needles

mermaid bag etui

Page 76

Kit contains: Fabrics, interfacings, interlining, buttons, mermaid charm, seed pearl, coral, sewing threads, embroidery threads and needles

tasmanian needle tidy

Page 86

Kit contains: Fabrics, interfacings, interlining, wool felt, button, sewing thread, embroidery threads and needles

holbein hexagon etui

Page 96

Kit contains: Fabrics, interfacings, interlining, comic board, wool felt, beading thread, sewing thread, embroidery threads, ribbon and needles

construction

CONSTRUCTION

bee contained etui

For colour photos and full details see pages 8–17.

cutting out

Where templates are not used, cut the pieces according to the measurements below.

Black silk dupion

Pincushion lining: cut one on the bias 5cm x 11.5cm (2" x 4½")

Cutting layout

Black silk dupion
1. Etui lining
2. Etui lid (2)
3. Etui base
4. Etui base lining
5. Needlebook (2)
6. Pincushion lining
7. Pincushion base
8. Ruler lining
9. Thread winder lining

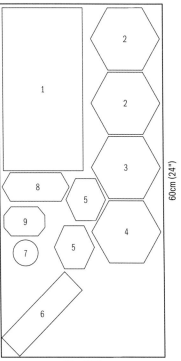

60cm (24")

30cm (12")

construction

All seam allowances are 13mm (½").

 right side of fabric   interlining

1. Preparing the embroidered linen

Remove any remaining tacking. Place the embroidered linen, face down, onto a soft, padded surface and press with a warm, dry iron, squaring the corners and straightening edges.

2. Making templates

Make a photocopy of each stitched piece and two copies of the needlebook covers, ruler and thread winder. Cut out one photocopy of each piece just inside the back stitch border. Cut out the second copies of the listed pieces just outside the back stitch border. These will be used as templates for cutting interfacing, interlining and board.

3. Preparing the lightweight fusible interfacing

Using the smaller photocopy templates, cut pieces of lightweight interfacing to fit inside the back stitch border of each stitched panel. When cutting the interfacing for the etui box panel, cut six pieces, one for each panel.

4. Applying the lightweight interfacing and cutting out the linen and silk lining

Position the pieces of lightweight interfacing, adhesive side down, over the wrong side of the stitched panels, checking to ensure that the interfacing sits just inside the back stitch outlines. Fuse in place. Attach one hexagon button at the position marked by the red hexagon on panel 3 of the etui using **D**.

Cut out each linen piece leaving a 13mm (½") seam allowance from the outline. Using the linen pieces as templates, cut a piece of silk lining for the etui box, needlebook front and back, ruler and thread winder.

5. Preparing the comic board and interlining

Use the ruler and craft knife to cut out the comic board and interlining and label each piece.

Using the photocopy templates, cut pieces of comic board to fit just inside the back stitch border of each etui box panel. Using the etui lid, base and base lining hexagon templates, cut one each of comic board. Cut one etui lid from the interlining.

For the etui box lining, cut one piece of interlining 12.3cm x 27cm wide (4¹³⁄₁₆" x 10⅝").

Using the smaller photocopy templates cut pieces of interlining for the needlebook front and back, scissor fob front and back, ruler front and thread winder front. Using the larger photocopy templates, cut two pieces of interlining for the needlebook lining and one piece for the ruler and thread winder lining.

6. Cords and tassels

Etui: using four, 45cm (18") lengths of **A**, make a 15cm (6") twisted cord.

Scissor fob: using three, 90cm (36") lengths of **A** and **B**, make a 30cm (12") two-colour twisted cord. Bind the knotted end of the cord securely with matching thread and trim away the knots (diag 1).

Bring both ends of the cord together and stitch securely (diag 2).

Using two, 60cm (24") lengths of **A** and **B**, make a 20cm (8") two-colour twisted cord for the tassel neck.

To make the tassel, wrap the piece of firm card with **A** until the skirt is the desired fullness. Cut the thread bundle at the base. Take one end of the bundle over the joined ends of the twisted cord (diag 3). Referring to the step-by-step instructions on page 107, wrap the small cord around the thread bundle to form the tassel neck. Trim the base of the skirt so that it is even.

....

7. ETUI

Preparing the etui box, lid and base

Position each comic board panel over the back of the respective embroidered panel and lace in place using sewing thread, taking each stitch under the back stitch lines on each side (diag 4).

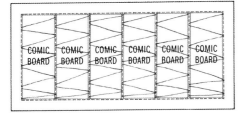

Mitre the corners of the linen and finger press. Press the corners with a dry iron. Fold in the seam allowance on each side, folding on the first linen thread outside the back stitch border. Finger press the seams then press with a dry iron. Stitch the mitres and lace the seam allowances along the long edges only, moving from panel to panel with running stitches along the upper or lower edge (diag 5).

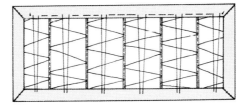

Measure and mark the halfway point on the upper and lower long edges of the interlining. Using the ruler and craft knife, score the interlining between the marked points. Measure across 4.6cm (1¹³⁄₁₆") to the right and mark on the upper and lower long edges. Score a line between the two marks in the same manner as before. Measure, mark and score again so that the right-hand side of the interlining is divided into three. The end section will be approximately 3mm (⅛") narrower than the preceding two sections. Repeat on the left-hand side of the interlining (diag 6).

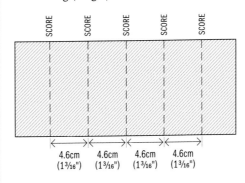

Centre the interlining, scored side uppermost, over the wrong side of the box lining piece and pin in place. Using the black beading thread, stitch the interlining to the lining along the scored lines with running stitch, taking small stitches into the silk and leaving long stitches on the interlining side.

Mitre and stitch the corners and fold in the seam allowances and press.

Using the comic board lid, base, base lining and interlining lid as templates and adding 13mm (½") seam allowance on each side, cut out the lid, lid lining, base and base lining from the silk. Centre the lid comic board over the wrong side of the lid silk. Fold in the seam allowance on each side and press. Stitch the folds in place at each corner and lace the seam allowances (diag 7).

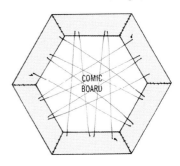

Repeat with the interlining and silk lid lining, comic board and silk base, and comic board and silk base lining.

Constructing the etui

Referring to the diagram, begin stitching the linen box panel to the base hexagon with joining stitch using the black beading thread and ensuring that the grain of the silk is running in the direction of the arrow (diag 8).

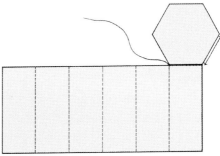

When completed, the grain of the silk should run parallel to the end of the title panel (panel 6). Continue stitching the sides of the base hexagon to the ends of the panels until a hexagonal cylinder is formed. Stitch the remaining edges of the cylinder together with joining stitch using **A** and the tapestry needle.

With the silk facing inwards, fold the lining panel until the end panels overlap and place inside the etui. Push the lining into place so that the overlapping edges meet in one of the corners behind panel 6. Using the black beading thread, stitch the silk lining to the linen along the open edges of the cylinder. Push the base lining panel down into the cylinder. At the centre of one side of the lid hexagon, stitch 13mm (½") of the looped end of the 15cm (6") twisted cord to the silk seam allowance (diag 9).

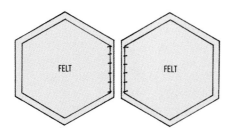

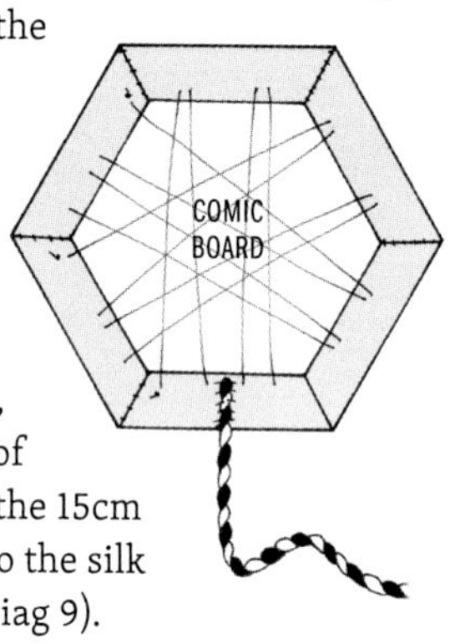

With wrong sides together and matching edges, stitch the lid lining to the lid using the black beading thread. Stitch the edge of the lid opposite the twisted cord to the end of panel 6 using the black beading thread. The twisted cord should be adjacent to the button. Attach the charms with the beading thread. Twist the cord around the button to close the etui.

....

8. NEEDLEBOOK

Preparing the needlebook

On each linen panel, mitre the corners, fold in the seam allowances and press. Open out the seams and position the interlining inside. Refold the corners and seams. Stitch the mitres. Prepare the silk lining pieces in the same manner. Using the template, cut two pieces of gold wool felt for the needlebook pages.

Constructing the needlebook

With wrong sides together and matching edges, stitch the silk lining panels to the linen panels with joining stitch using the black beading thread. Position each gold felt page over the lining and stitch in place as shown using the beading thread (diag 10).

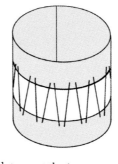

To make the spine, place the two covers together, linen side outermost, and hold in place with an elastic band so that the

aligned edges where the felt pages have been attached are accessible. These are the edges that will be joined. Press the length of **E**. Thread each end of the ribbon into a tapestry needle. Beginning at the upper edge on one side, take one end of the ribbon through the first back stitch on the back cover and the other end through the first back stitch on the front cover (diag 11).

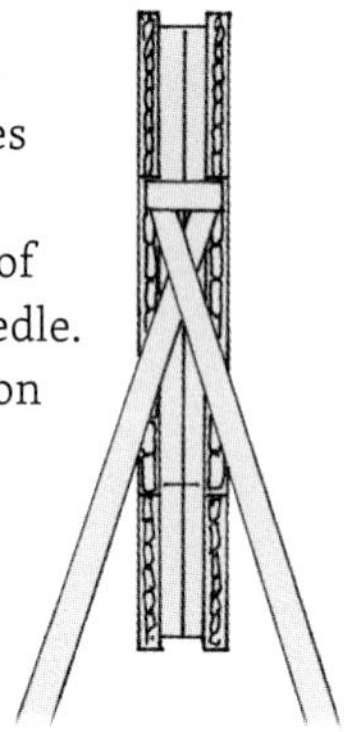

Take care to ensure that the ribbon is centred and remains flat. Working in the same manner as lacing up shoes, cross the ribbons taking them through every back stitch on the opposite sides. Continue working in this manner to the end. After threading the ribbons through the last back stitch on each side, remove the needles and tie the ribbon tails into a bow. Trim away any excess ribbon and cut the ends at a 45 degree angle.

....

9. PINCUSHION

Preparing the pincushion

On the embroidered panel, mitre the corners, fold in the seam allowances and press. Stitch the mitres. Fold in 13mm (½") at one short end of the silk bias strip and press. Centre the strip inside the plastic cylinder, ensuring that the folded end covers the raw end. Fold the long edges of the silk over the exterior of the cylinder and lace as shown using the beading thread (diag 12).

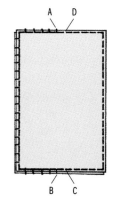

Using the circle templates, cut the interlining and silk base. Leaving a tail at each end, work a line of gathering 3mm (⅛") in from the raw edge on the pincushion base silk. Centre the base interlining circle over

the wrong side of the silk and pull up the gathering threads. Secure the threads and press the gathers.

Cut a 4cm x 42cm wide (1⅝" x 16½") strip of gold felt. At one short end measure up 2.9cm (1⅛") from the lower edge and mark with the fabric marker. At the second short end measure up 3.5cm (1⅜") and mark. Rule a line between the two marks with the fabric marker and ruler and cut along the marked line (diag 13).

Constructing the pincushion

Wrap the prepared linen around the cylinder and stitch the short ends together with joining stitch using **A**. Position the silk base and stitch in place through the lower edge of the linen using the black beading thread.

Beginning at the taller end, roll up the felt as tightly as possible, keeping the lower edge straight. Stitch the short end in place with matching thread to secure the roll. Push the flat end of the roll down into the covered cylinder. Push the shank of the bee button down into the centre of the roll and stitch in place using matching thread.

....

10. SCISSOR FOB

Preparing the scissor fob

On each linen piece mitre the corners, fold in the seam allowance and press. Open out the seams and position the interlining inside. Refold the corners and seams. Trim the seam allowance if necessary and stitch the mitres. Press.

Constructing the scissor fob

With wrong sides together and matching edges, stitch the fob pieces together with joining stitch between A and B using **A** (diag 14).

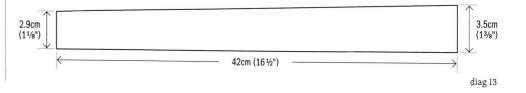

2.9cm (1⅛")   3.5cm (1⅜")

42cm (16½")

diag 13

Open the panels and place the cord, tassel end down, between them. Close the panels and continue stitching from C to D, taking care not to catch the cord as this will prevent it from sliding. Attach the looped end of the cord to a pair of embroidery scissors.

11. RULER

Preparing the ruler

On the linen panel, mitre the corners, fold in the seam allowance and press. Open out the seams and position the interlining inside. Refold the corners and seams. Trim the seam allowance if necessary and stitch the mitres. Prepare the silk lining piece in the same manner.

Constructing the ruler

With wrong sides together and matching edges, stitch the lining to the linen with joining stitch using the black beading thread.

12. THREAD WINDER

Preparing the thread winder

On the linen panel, mitre the corners, fold in the seam allowance and press. Open out the seams and position the interlining inside. Refold the corners and seams. Trim the seam allowance if necessary and stitch the mitres. Prepare the silk lining piece in a similar manner. Before joining the lining to the linen, sew the remaining hexagon button in place approximately 6mm (¼") from one end of the lining panel using **D** (diag 15).

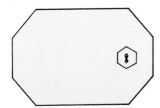

Constructing the thread winder

With wrong sides together and matching edges, stitch the lining to the linen with joining stitch using the black beading thread.

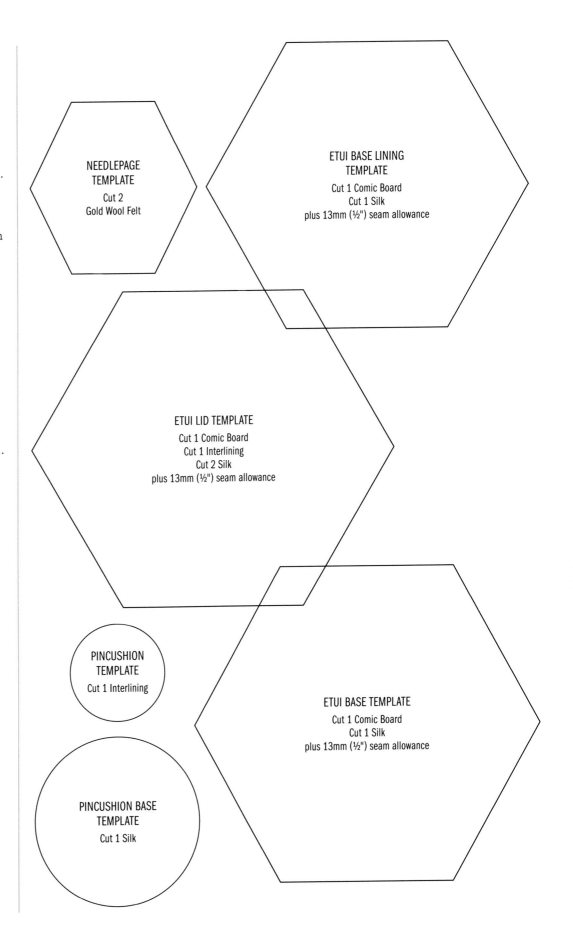

NEEDLEPAGE
TEMPLATE

Cut 2
Gold Wool Felt

ETUI BASE LINING
TEMPLATE

Cut 1 Comic Board
Cut 1 Silk
plus 13mm (½") seam allowance

ETUI LID TEMPLATE

Cut 1 Comic Board
Cut 1 Interlining
Cut 2 Silk
plus 13mm (½") seam allowance

PINCUSHION
TEMPLATE

Cut 1 Interlining

ETUI BASE TEMPLATE

Cut 1 Comic Board
Cut 1 Silk
plus 13mm (½") seam allowance

PINCUSHION BASE
TEMPLATE

Cut 1 Silk

gathering for winter etui

For colour photos and full details see pages 18-29.

cutting out

Where templates are not used, cut the pieces according to the measurements below.

Copper silk dupion

Etui base side lining: cut one on the bias 11cm x 25cm (4⅜" x 10")

Etui lid side lining: cut one on the bias 9cm x 25cm (3½" x 10")

Pincushion side lining: cut one on the bias 5cm x 11.5cm (2" x 4½")

Cutting layout

Copper silk dupion

1. Base side lining
2. Lid side lining
3. Base lining
4. Lid lining
5. Pincushion side lining
6. Pincushion base
7. Needlebook (2)
8. Scissor sheath (2)

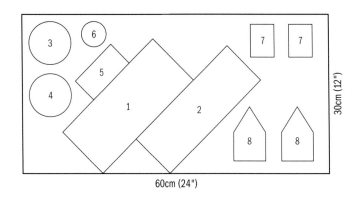

construction

All seam allowances are 13mm (½").

 right side of fabric

1. Preparing the embroidered linen

Remove any remaining tacking. Place the embroidered linen, face down, onto a soft, padded surface and press with a warm, dry iron, squaring the corners and straightening edges.

2. Making templates

Make a photocopy of each stitched piece. Cut out each photocopy just inside the back stitch outline. These will be used as templates for cutting interfacing and interlining.

3. Preparing the lightweight fusible interfacing

Using the photocopy templates, cut pieces of lightweight interfacing to fit inside the back stitch border of each stitched panel. Using the linen circle template, cut two pieces of interfacing for the lid and base.

4. Applying the lightweight interfacing and cutting out the linen and silk lining

Position the pieces of lightweight interfacing, adhesive side down, over the wrong side of the stitched panels, checking to ensure that the interfacing sits just inside the back stitch outlines. Fuse in place. Centre the interfacing circles over the wrong side of the lid and base embroidery and fuse in place.

Cut out each linen piece leaving a 13mm (½") seam allowance from the outline. Cut out the lid and base leaving a 13mm

(½") seam allowance from the edge of the interfacing. Using the linen pieces as templates, cut a piece of silk lining for the scissor sheath front and back and needlebook front and back. Using the lining circle template, cut out two circles of silk, adding a 13mm (½") seam allowance.

5. Preparing the interlining and wadding

Use the ruler and craft knife to cut out the interlining and label each piece.

Using the photocopy templates cut pieces of interlining for the scissor sheath front and back, needlebook front and back and scissor fob front and back. Using the linen circle template cut three interlining circles and one wadding circle. Put two interlining circles aside. Using the lining circle template cut two interlining circles. On one linen-size interlining circle, the wadding circle and the two interlining circles cut with the lining circle template, rule perpendicular lines across the centre of each circle. Where the lines intersect, cut out a small diamond (diag 1).

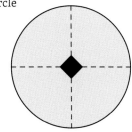

6. Cords and tassels

Etui: using six, 1.85m (2yd) lengths of **A**, make a 61cm (24") twisted cord. At each end of the cord, coat 1cm (⅜") with a layer of craft glue, rubbing it into the thread. Allow to dry.

Scissor sheath: Using three, 45cm (18") lengths of **A** for each one, make two 15cm (6") twisted cords.

Scissor fob: using six, 90cm (36") lengths of **A**, make a 30cm (12") twisted cord. Bind the knotted end of the cord securely with matching thread and trim away the knots (diag 2).

Bring both ends of the cord together and stitch securely (diag 3).

Using four, 60cm (24") lengths of **A** make a 20cm (8") twisted cord for the tassel neck.

To make the tassel, wrap the piece of firm card with **A** until the skirt is the desired fullness. Cut the thread bundle at the base. Take one end of the bundle over the joined ends of the twisted cord (diag 4).

Referring to the step-by-step instructions on page 107, wrap the small cord around the thread bundle to form the tassel neck. Trim the base of the skirt so that it is even.

....

7. ETUI

Preparing the etui lid and base

Leaving a tail at each end and using the beading thread, work a line of gathering around each linen and silk circle, 6mm (¼") in from the raw edge. Centre the circle of wadding over the wrong side of the linen lid piece. Position the linen-size interlining with the centre hole over the wadding and pull up the gathering thread firmly and tie off. Press the gathers. Centre the two remaining linen-size interlining circles over the wrong side of the linen base piece, pull up the gathers, secure the thread and press as before. Prepare the silk lining and remaining circles of interlining in a similar manner, placing one interlining circle over the wrong side of each silk piece.

Preparing the etui and etui lid sides

Mitre the corners, fold in the seam allowances, folding on the first linen thread outside the back stitch border, and finger press each linen side panel. Stitch the mitres and press the edges.

For the etui base you need to cut pieces of Mylar® that are approximately 6.7cm x 21cm wide (2⅝" x 8¼") and 6.7cm x 20.9cm wide (2⅝" x 8³⁄₁₆"). Measure the depth of the stitched linen base and adjust the 6.7cm (2⅝") measurement as necessary. Be very precise. Cut two pieces of adhesive tape 10cm (4") long. Bring the short ends of one piece together and butt against one another, forming a tube. Tape the join on the outside and fold the extending ends of the tape to the inside (diag 5).

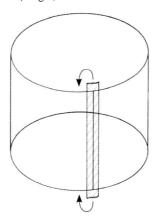

Repeat with the second, slightly smaller piece. With the joins on opposing sides of the cylinder, slide the smaller piece down inside the larger piece and line up the upper and lower edges (diag 6).

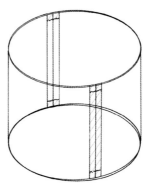

For the etui lid you need to cut pieces of Mylar® that are approximately 3.7cm x 21cm wide (1½" x 8¼") and 3.7cm x 20.9cm wide (1½" x 8³⁄₁₆"). Measure the depth of the stitched linen lid and adjust the 3.7cm (1½") measurement as necessary. Join the pieces and assemble in the same manner as the base.

At one short end of each large silk bias strip, fold under 13mm (½") and press. With the folded edge to the inside, roll the larger strip into a loose tube and place inside the larger cylinder. Centre the silk in the cylinder, ensuring that the folded short end covers the raw short end and the fabric is firm to the cylinder. Fold the long edges of the silk over the exterior of the cylinder and lace as shown using the beading thread (diag 7).

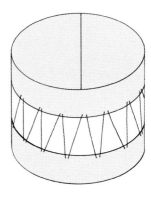

Repeat with the smaller silk strip and cylinder.

Constructing the etui

Wrap each piece of linen around the respective lined cylinder and stitch the short edges together using joining stitch and **A**. Attach an amber crystal bead to the seam of the base cylinder, just below the top edge (diag 8).

Attach the second amber bead at the centre front of the base cylinder, just below the top edge. At the corresponding points on the lid sides, work a Hedebo stitch loop using **A**.

Position the linen lid on the upper edge of the lid cylinder and stitch in place with joining stitch using **A**. Push one prepared silk lining disc into the inside of the lid. Using the dressmaker's awl, carefully open the eyelet at the centre of the lid, pushing the awl down through the lid lining panel to open a hole in the silk. The hole needs to be large enough for both ends of the etui cord to pass through.

Trim away any knots at the ends of the twisted cord. The glue applied earlier should make the ends of the cord firm. Thread one end of the twisted cord through the hole in the stem of the wooden acorn. Bring the cord ends together and slide the acorn to the centre of the cord. Thread each end of the cord through one hole of the hexagonal button then down through the eyelet and the hole in the lid and lid lining. Using the dressmaker's awl, pierce a hole through the centre of the base lining piece. Take the cords through the silk base lining then down through the centre of the base cylinder. Leaving 1cm (⅜") tails, stitch the ends of the cord to the centre of the interlining on the linen base, taking care not to go through the linen (diag 9).

Using joining stitch and **A**, stitch the base to the lower edge of the base cylinder. Slide the silk base lining down the cord into the base of the cylinder.

8. SCISSOR SHEATH

Preparing the scissor sheath

On each linen panel, mitre the corners, fold in the seam allowances and press. Open out the seams and position the interlining inside. Refold the corners and seams. Stitch the mitres. Using the prepared linen panels as templates, cut two pieces of medium weight fusible interfacing. Trim 1mm-2mm (¹⁄₁₆") off each side. Centre each piece of interfacing on the wrong side of a silk lining piece and fuse in place. Mitre the corners, fold in the seam allowance and press. Stitch the mitres.

Constructing the scissor sheath

Attach 1cm (⅜") at one end of each twisted cord to the seam allowance at the centre of each linen panel. With wrong sides together and matching the short straight edges, ladder stitch each lining piece to one linen panel along the short straight edge only using the beading thread (diag 10).

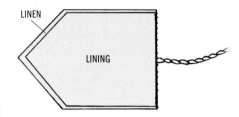

With the lining sides together and matching edges, stitch the linen panels together around the outer edge with joining stitch using **A**, leaving the short straight edges open.

9. NEEDLEBOOK

Preparing the needlebook

On each linen panel, mitre the corners, fold in the seam allowances and press. Open out the seams and position the interlining inside. Refold the corners and seams. Stitch the mitres. Using the prepared linen panels as templates, cut two pieces of medium weight fusible interfacing. Trim 1mm-2mm (¹⁄₁₆") off each side. Centre each piece of interfacing on the wrong side of a silk lining piece and fuse in place. Mitre the corners, fold in the seam allowance and press. Stitch the mitres.

Using the linen panels as a guide, cut two pieces of gold wool felt, slightly smaller than the linen, for the needlebook pages.

Constructing the needlebook

With wrong sides together and matching edges, stitch the silk lining panels to the linen panels with joining stitch using the beading thread. Position each gold felt page over the lining and stitch in place as shown using the beading thread (diag 11).

To make the spine, place the two covers together, linen side outermost, and hold in place with an elastic band so that the aligned edges where the felt pages have been attached are accessible. These are the two edges that will be joined. Press the length of **J**. Thread each end of the ribbon into a tapestry needle. Beginning at the lower edge on one side, take one end of the ribbon through the first back stitch on the back cover and the other end through the first back stitch on the front cover (diag 12).

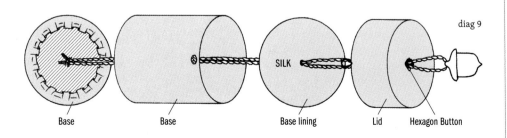

Base   Base   Base lining   Lid   Hexagon Button

diag 9

Take care to ensure that the ribbon is centred and remains flat. Working in the same manner as lacing up shoes, cross the ribbons and take them through every back stitch on opposite sides. Continue working in this manner to the end. After threading the ribbons through the last back stitch on each side, remove the needles and tie the ribbon tails into a bow. Trim away any excess ribbon and cut the ends at a 45 degree angle.

....

10. PINCUSHION

Preparing the pincushion

On the embroidered panel, mitre the corners, fold in the seam allowances and press. Stitch the mitres. Fold in 13mm (½") at one short end of the silk bias strip and press. Centre the strip inside the plastic cylinder, ensuring that the folded end covers the raw end. Fold the long edges of the silk over the exterior of the cylinder and lace as shown using the beading thread (diag 13).

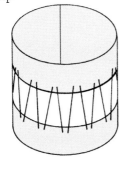

Leaving a tail at each end, work a line of gathering 3mm (⅛") in from the raw edge on the pincushion base silk. Centre the base interlining circle over the wrong side of the silk and pull up the gathering threads. Secure the threads and press the gathers.

Cut a 4cm x 42cm wide (1⅝" x 16½") strip of green felt. At one short end measure up 2.9cm (1⅛") from the lower edge and mark with the fabric marker. At the second short end measure up 3.5cm (1⅜") and mark. Rule a line between the two marks with the fabric marker and ruler and cut along the marked line (diag 14).

Constructing the pincushion

Wrap the prepared linen around the cylinder and stitch the short ends together with joining stitch using **A**. Position the silk base and stitch in place through the lower edge of the linen using the beading thread.

Beginning at the taller end, roll up the felt as tightly as possible, keeping the lower edge straight. Stitch the short end in place with matching thread to secure the roll. Push the flat end of the roll down into the covered cylinder.

....

10. SCISSOR FOB

Preparing the scissor fob

On each linen piece mitre the corners, fold in the seam allowance and press. Open out the seams and position the interlining inside. Refold the corners and seams. Trim the seam allowance if necessary and stitch the mitres. Press.

Constructing the scissor fob.

With wrong sides together and matching edges, stitch the fob pieces together with joining stitch between A and B using **A** (diag 15).

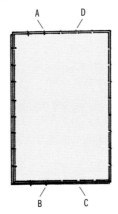

Open the panels and place the cord, tassel end down, between them. Close the panels and continue stitching from C to D, taking care not to catch the cord as this will prevent it from sliding. Attach the looped end of the cord to a pair of embroidery scissors.

PINCUSHION TEMPLATE
Cut 1 Interlining

PINCUSHION BASE TEMPLATE
Cut 1 Silk

LID AND BASE LINING TEMPLATE
Cut 2 Interlining
Cut 2 Silk
plus 13mm (½") seam allowance

LINEN LID AND BASE TEMPLATE
Cut 1 Wadding
Cut 3 Interlining
Cut 2 Interfacing

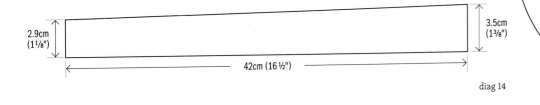

2.9cm (1⅛")   3.5cm (1⅜")

42cm (16½")

diag 14

CONSTRUCTION

virgin queen's stitching pocket

For colour photos and full details see pages 30–37.

cutting out

Where templates are not used, cut the pieces according to the measurements below.

Willow green silk dupion

Stitching pocket lining: cut one 10cm x 39.5cm wide (4" x 15½")

construction

All seam allowances are 13mm (½").

 right side of fabric   interfacing   interlining

1. Preparing the embroidered linen

Remove any remaining tacking. Place the embroidered linen, face down, onto a soft, padded surface and press with a warm, dry iron, squaring the corners and straightening edges.

2. Making templates

Omitting the needlepage, make a photocopy of each stitched piece. Label and cut out the photocopy of each piece just inside the outer back stitch outline, leaving the front, spine and back stitching pocket template as one piece.

These will be used as templates for cutting interfacing and interlining.

3. Preparing the lightweight fusible interfacing

Using the templates, cut pieces of lightweight interfacing to fit inside the back stitch outline of each scissor fob panel. Cut a long rectangle of lightweight interfacing for the front, spine and back panels to fit inside the back stitch outline along the outer edges, covering the seam allowances in the spine area (diag 1).

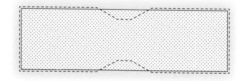

4. Applying the lightweight interfacing and cutting out the linen

Position the pieces of lightweight interfacing, adhesive side down, over the wrong side of the stitched panels, checking to ensure that the interfacing sits just inside the back stitch outlines. The rectangle for the front, spine and back panels will cover the seam allowances as in diagram 1. Fuse in place.

Cut out each piece, leaving a 13mm (½") seam allowance from the back stitch outlines.

5. Preparing the medium weight interfacing

Using the photocopy template of the stitching pocket panel, cut a piece of medium weight interfacing to fit the panel.

6. Preparing the interlining

Cut the photocopy template of the stitching pocket into three sections, one each for the front, spine and back, cutting inside the back stitch lines on each panel (diag 2).

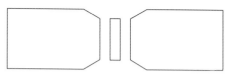

Using the photocopy templates, ruler and craft knife, cut and label a piece of interlining to fit each stitched panel, including the scissor fob, checking to ensure that each piece fits inside the back stitch outlines. You should have three pieces for the stitching pocket and two pieces for the scissor fob.

7. Cords and tassel

Pocket: using six, 168cm (66") lengths of **A**, make a 56cm (22") twisted cord.

Scissor fob: using six 90cm (36") lengths of **A**, make a 30cm (12") twisted cord. Bind the knotted end of the cord securely with matching thread and trim away the knots. Bring both ends of the cord together and stitch securely (diag 3).

Using four, 60cm (24") lengths of **A**, make a 20cm (8") twisted cord for the tassel neck.

To make the tassel, wrap the piece of firm card with **A** until the skirt is the desired fullness. Cut the thread bundle at the base. Take one end of the bundle over the joined ends of the twisted cord (diag 4).

Referring to the step-by-step instructions on page 107, wrap the small cord around the thread bundle to form the tassel neck. Trim the base of the skirt so that it is even.

8. POCKET

Preparing the linen panels

Work a Hedebo stitch loop at each side of the upper edge of the front panel, working over the third and fourth back stitches from each side and using **A**. Each loop should be large enough for a twisted cord to pass through.

Position the small piece of interlining cut for the spine panel over the wrong side of the base panel on the linen and lace in place using the beading thread, taking each stitch under the back stitch lines on each side.

Clip into the seam allowance at the upper and lower edges of the spine. Do not cut right to the back stitches, leaving two fabric threads uncut (diag 5).

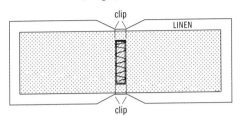

Mitre the corners of the linen and finger press. Press the corners with a dry iron. Fold in the seam allowance on each side, folding on the first linen thread outside the back stitch border. Finger press the seams then press with a dry iron. Open out the seams and position the front and back interlining pieces over the back of the panels. Refold the corners and seams. Stitch the mitres and lace the seam allowances along the long edges only (diag 6).

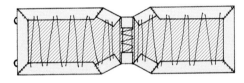

Preparing the lining and internal pocket

Place the silk rectangle for the lining on a flat surface right side uppermost. Measure in 10cm (4") from the right-hand short edge. At this point fold the fabric under and press (diag 7).

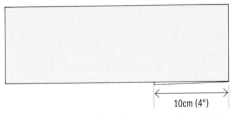

10cm (4")

Measure in 6.5cm (2½") from the first fold and fold the fabric to the right side (diag 8).

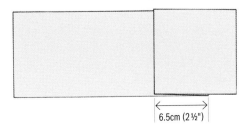

6.5cm (2½")

Press and turn to the wrong side. Centre the medium weight interfacing, adhesive side down, over the folded lining (diag 9).

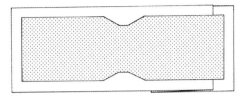

Fuse in place.

Turn the silk to the right side. If desired, lightly mark a line to divide the pocket into two. Using **C**, work tiny running stitch along the line, reinforcing with extra stitches at each end (diag 10).

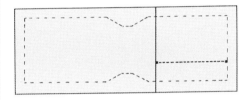

Trim the seam allowances in the spine panel area to follow the shape of the interfacing and clip at each side of the base area (diag 11).

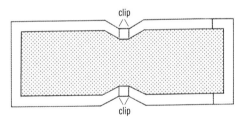

Mitre the corners of the silk lining and fold in the seam allowance. Press the corners and edges and stitch the mitres.

Attaching the needlepage

Clip and remove the first fabric thread outside the nun stitch border. Cut out the needlepage along the withdrawn thread lines, cutting as close as possible to the stitches.

With right sides facing up, centre the needlepage over the side of the lining without the pocket, with one short edge of the page 13mm (½") from the short edge of the lining. Using the beading thread and **K**, attach the two corners nearest the short edge of the lining to the silk, stitching through all layers (diag 12).

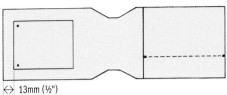

13mm (½")

Constructing the pocket

With wrong sides together, position the silk lining over the linen panel. The lining should be slightly smaller than the linen. Pin in place. Using ladder stitch and the beading thread, and beginning at the upper corner for the back panel, ladder stitch the lining to the linen around three sides, working along the first long end, the short end with the Hedebo stitch loops, and along the remaining long end.

Begin to ladder stitch the remaining short side closed, as far as the third back stitch. Insert 13mm (½") of one end of the twisted cord into the seam opening and position it over the linen seam allowance between the third and fourth back stitches. Stitch the cord securely to the linen, stitching back and forth through the cord, linen and lining a few times. Take the remaining

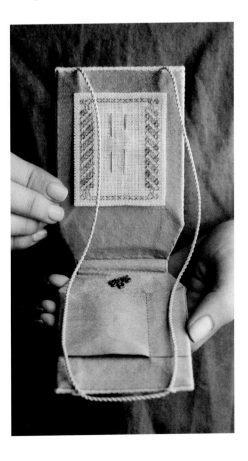

end of the cord and thread it through the corresponding Hedebo stitch loop, from inside to outside, and through the second loop from outside to inside. Bring the cord back to the open seam and tack 13mm (½") of the end of the cord at the mirror position to the first end (diag 13).

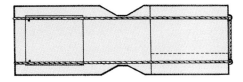

Ladder stitch the remaining seam closed, stitching through the cord to secure as before.

To close the pocket, pull the twisted cord upwards.

9. SCISSOR FOB

Preparing the scissor fob

On each linen piece mitre the corners, fold in the seam allowance and press. Open out the seams and position the interlining inside. Refold the corners and seams. Trim the seam allowance if necessary and stitch the mitres. Press.

Constructing the scissor fob

Using **A**, with wrong sides together and matching edges, stitch the fob pieces together with joining stitch between A and B (diag 14).

Open the panels and place the cord, tassel end down, between them. Close the panels and continue stitching from C to D, taking care not to catch the cord as this will prevent it from sliding. Attach the looped end of the cord to a pair of embroidery scissors.

bristol bag etui

For colour photos and full details see pages 38–47.

cutting out

Where pattern pieces are not provided, cut the pieces according to the measurements below.

Red cotton

Bag lining and top: cut two, each 26.3cm x 16.5cm wide (10⅜" x 6½")

construction

All seam allowances are 13mm (½") unless otherwise specified.

 right side of fabric   interfacing

1. Preparing the embroidered linen

Remove any remaining tacking. Place the embroidered linen, face down, onto a soft, padded surface and press with a warm, dry iron, squaring the corners and straightening edges.

2. Making templates

Make a photocopy of each stitched piece and two copies of the needlebook covers and thread winder. Cut out one photocopy of each piece just inside the back stitch border. These will be used as templates for cutting interfacing and comic board. Cut out the second copies of the listed pieces just outside the back stitch border. These will be used as templates for cutting comic board.

3. Preparing the lightweight fusible interfacing

Using the photocopy templates, cut pieces of lightweight interfacing to fit inside the back stitch border of each stitched panel. Using the octagon template, cut a piece of interfacing for the base.

4. Applying the lightweight interfacing and cutting out the linen and cotton print lining

Position the pieces of lightweight interfacing, adhesive side down, over the wrong side of the stitched panels, checking to ensure that the interfacing sits just inside the back stitch outlines. Fuse in place. Centre the octagon of interfacing over the etui base embroidery, ensuring that the straight edges run along the grainlines of the fabric and fuse in place.

Cut out each linen piece leaving a 13mm (½") seam allowance from the outline. Using the linen pieces as templates, cut pieces of cotton print lining for the needlebook front and back, and thread winder.

5. Preparing the comic board

Use the ruler and craft knife to cut out the comic board and label each piece.

Using the photocopy templates, cut and label pieces of comic board to fit just inside the back stitch border of the needlebook front and back panels, thread winder and scissor fob front and back panels. Using the octagon template, cut one for the etui base. Using the second photocopy templates, cut and label pieces of comic board for the needlebook front and back lining and the thread winder lining.

6. Preparing the patchwork shapes

Use pre-cut paper piecing triangles or cut sixteen 3.2cm (1¼") triangles for the bag and eight 3.8cm (1½") triangles for the pincushion from the paper, using the triangle templates.

Cut each 7.5cm x 38cm wide (3" x 15") strip of red and white print cotton into six even pieces, each one measuring approximately 6.5cm x 5.7 cm wide (2½" x 2¼"). Centre one paper triangle on the wrong side of one fabric piece and trim the fabric to leave a 1cm (⅜") seam allowance (diag 1).

Thread the milliner's needle with a length of red sewing thread and knot the end. Fold the seam allowance on one edge over the paper template and hold securely. Fold a second edge over the paper template, overlapping the first and hold in place with two tacking stitches at the corner through the fabric only. Fold the remaining seam allowance over the template as shown. Work running stitch along the second folded edge and tack

the third edge in place at the corner. Work running stitch along the third folded edge and tack the third edge to the first edge at the corner (diag 2).

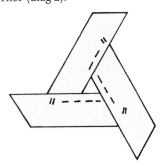

Turn to the right side. Do not trim away the fabric tabs at the corners (diag 3).

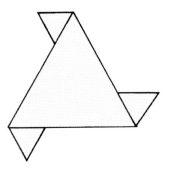

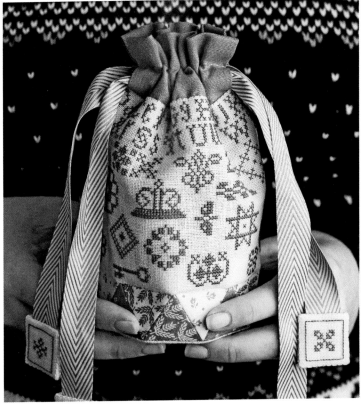

Repeat with the remaining fabric pieces and paper templates so that you have four small triangles and two larger triangles in each of the four fabrics.

7. Cords and tassels

Etui lining: Using four, 100cm (39") lengths of **A** make a 33cm (13") twisted cord.

Scissor fob: using six, 122cm (48") lengths of **A** make a 40cm (16") twisted cord. Using four, 60cm (24") lengths of **A** make a 20cm (8") twisted cord for the tassel neck. Bind the knotted end of the 40cm (16") cord to secure and trim away the knots. Bring the bound and looped ends of the cord together and stitch securely (diag 4).

To make the tassel, wrap the piece of firm card with **A** until the skirt is the desired fullness. Cut the thread bundle at the base. Take one end of the bundle over the joined ends of the twisted cord. Referring to the step-by-step instructions on page 107, wrap the 20cm (8") cord around the thread bundle to form the tassel neck. Trim the base of the skirt so that it is even.

. . . .

8. ETUI

Preparing the patchwork band

The sixteen bag triangles are stitched together in a long strip, alternating fabrics with red and white backgrounds. With right sides together and matching edges, whip stitch two triangles together using the red sewing thread, working approximately eight stitches and a double stitch at the beginning and end of the edge. Unfold the first two triangles and stitch a third triangle in place in the same manner (diag 5).

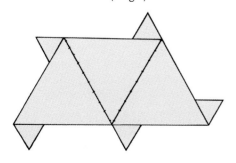

Continue working in this manner until all triangles are stitched.

Preparing the etui base

Using the edges of the interfacing as a guide, fold in each seam allowance and press. Open out the seams and position the comic board inside. Refold the seam allowance and corners. Stitch each corner and lace the seam allowances firmly over the board (diag 6).

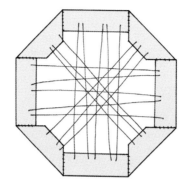

Constructing the etui

Line up the patchwork band and base of the linen panel.

> **NOTE** *The band and base should be the same length but if the paper piecing is a little too tight or too loose, you may need to adjust the length of the panel. To adjust the length, remove the vertical back stitch border lines and move them in or out as required. This is not difficult to do and is crucial to the construction of the bag.*

With right sides together and matching the edge of the patchwork band and the back stitch outline, stitch the pieces together with ladder stitch using the white beading thread and tucking the corner tabs of each triangle to the back (diag 7).

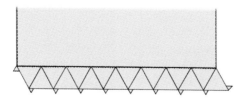

Attach the base to the lower edge of the patchwork panel using ladder stitch and the white beading thread, tucking the corner tabs of each triangle to the back and taking

care to align each side of the octagon with the base of a patchwork triangle. Do not end off the thread (diag 8).

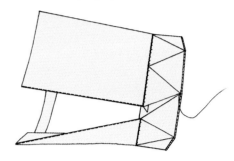

Once the last base and band edges are joined, stitch the two end triangles together.

Using **A**, stitch the etui back seam with joining stitch.

To prepare the lining, fold 1.5cm (⅝") to the back down each long edge and press (fold A). Fold under 6mm (¼") along the upper short edge and press (fold B) and 1cm (⅜") along the lower short edge and press (fold C). On the upper short edge, measure down 4cm (1⅝") from the folded edge, fold to the back and press (fold D). Measure down another 4cm (1⅝") from the second fold and mark on the long edges only (diag 9).

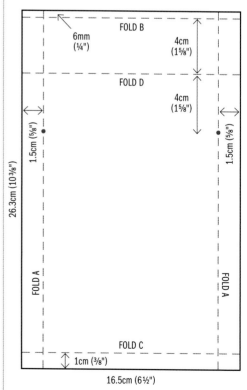

Repeat on the second piece of lining fabric. Open out all the folds. With right sides together and matching raw edges, stitch the two pieces together along one long edge with running stitch from the base to the mark, working along the fold creases and using the red sewing thread (diag 10).

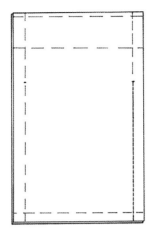

Carefully press the seam open. With the wrong side uppermost, refold the seam allowance on the remaining long sides and the two folds along the upper short edge. Press. Measure down 2cm (¾") from the upper fold and mark a line across the fabric with the ruler and air-soluble fabric marker. Pin in place. Using the red sewing thread, work a line of small running stitches across the marked line on one half of the lining, through both layers of fabric. Slip stitch the lower fold in place on one side (diag 11).

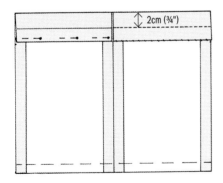

Repeat on the remaining half to complete the ribbon casing.

Measure up and fold 3mm (⅛") from the lower raw edge. Unfold and place the twisted cord for the lining just inside the second fold crease at the lower fold. Refold the casing, ensuring that the cord is inside

the second fold and the ends extend beyond the fabric on each side (diag 12).

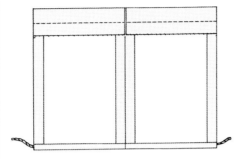

Using the red sewing thread, work small running stitch across the fabric close to the top fold, taking care not to catch the cord (diag 13).

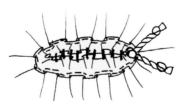

With right sides together and matching edges, overcast the remaining folded long edges together, from the top of the cord casing to the base of the ribbon casing using the red sewing thread (diag 14).

Pull up the cord firmly and tie off tightly. Knot the ends of the cord close to the knot and trim away the excess. Stitch the edges of the fabric together to close the remaining small hole (diag 15).

Mark the centre of one lining panel with a pin. Aligning the pin with the centre of the etui panel, slide the lining down into the bag. With the upper edge of the etui linen aligned with the lower edge of the ribbon casing, pin the layers together and stitch with ladder stitch using the red sewing thread.

Preparing the ribbon tabs

Trim the seam allowance if desired. On each tab, mitre the corners, fold in the seam allowance and press. Stitch the mitres.

Cut the length of chevron twill ribbon in half. Fold in and press 13mm (½") at each end of each ribbon. Thread one ribbon through the casing beginning and ending on the right-hand side of the bag and the second ribbon beginning and ending on the left-hand side of the bag. Stitch each end of each ribbon to the back of a tab with a geometric design (diag 16).

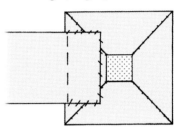

Positioning the two initial tabs on one side of the bag and the two date tabs on the other side, stitch the initial and date tabs to the geometric tabs with joining stitch using **A**, working through the ribbon at the top edge of each tab.

....

9. NEEDLEBOOK

Preparing the needlebook

On each linen panel, mitre the corners, fold in the seam allowances and press. Open out the seams and position the comic board inside. Refold the corners and seams. Stitch the mitres. Prepare the cotton lining pieces in the same manner. Cut two pieces of red wool felt, 5.5cm x 4cm wide (2¼" x 1⅝") for the needlebook pages.

Constructing the needlebook

With wrong sides together and matching edges, stitch the cotton lining panels to the linen panels with joining stitch using the white beading thread. Position each felt page over the lining and stitch in place as shown using the red sewing thread (diag 17).

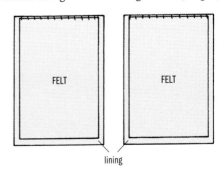

To make the spine, place the two covers together, linen side outermost, and hold in place with an elastic band so that the long edges are accessible. Press the length of **C**. Thread each end of the ribbon into a tapestry needle. Beginning at the lower edge on one side, take one end of the ribbon through the first back stitch on the back cover and the other end through the first back stitch on the front cover (diag 18).

Take care to ensure that the ribbon is centred and remains flat. Working in the same manner as lacing up shoes, cross the ribbons and take them through every back stitch on the opposite sides. Continue working in this manner to the end. After threading the ribbons through the last back stitch on each side, remove the needles and tie the ribbon tails into a bow. Trim away any excess ribbon and cut the ends at a 45 degree angle.

10. PINCUSHION

Working in a similar manner to the bag band, whip stitch the larger triangles together following the diagram and alternating the red and white background fabrics (diag 19).

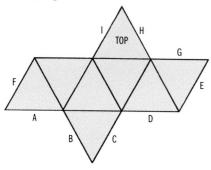

Following the alphabetical sequence, ladder stitch side A to side B, side C to side D and side E to side F. Fill the pincushion with fibre-fill. If desired, weight the pincushion by filling halfway, adding one or two coins or metal washers then adding the remainder of the filling. Ladder stitch side G to side H, add additional fibre-fill if required then stitch side I to side J to complete the octahedron.

11. SCISSOR FOB

Preparing the scissor fob

On each linen piece mitre the corners, fold in the seam allowance and press. Open out the seams and position the comic board inside. Refold the corners and seams and stitch the mitres. Press.

Constructing the scissor fob

With wrong sides facing and using **A**, stitch the panels together with joining stitch from A to B (diag 20).

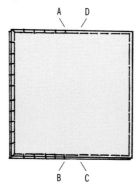

Open the panels and place the cord, tassel side down, between them. Close the panels and continue stitching from C to D, taking care not to catch the cords as this will prevent them from sliding. Attach the looped end of the cord to a pair of embroidery scissors.

12. THREAD WINDER

Preparing the thread winder

On the linen panel, mitre the corners, fold in the seam allowances and press. Open out the seams and position the comic board inside. Refold the corners and seams. Trim the seam allowance if necessary and stitch the mitres. Prepare the cotton lining piece in a similar manner. Before positioning the comic board, sew the red button in place approximately 1cm (⅜") from one folded end of the lining panel (diag 21).

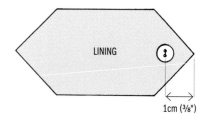

Constructing the thread winder

With wrong sides together and matching edges, stitch the cotton lining to the linen with joining stitch using the white beading thread.

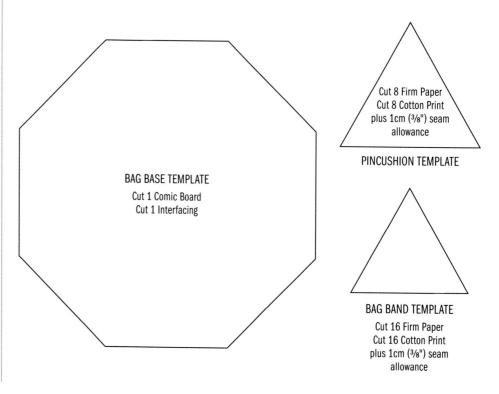

BAG BASE TEMPLATE
Cut 1 Comic Board
Cut 1 Interfacing

PINCUSHION TEMPLATE

Cut 8 Firm Paper
Cut 8 Cotton Print
plus 1cm (⅜") seam allowance

BAG BAND TEMPLATE
Cut 16 Firm Paper
Cut 16 Cotton Print
plus 1cm (⅜") seam allowance

CONSTRUCTION

exact change etui

For colour photos and full details see pages 48–59.

cutting out

Cutting layout

Parrot green silk dupion

1. Etui base
2. Etui sides (2)
3. Needlebook (2)
4. Waxer box base
5. Waxer box sides (2)

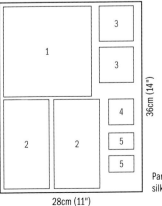

36cm (14")

28cm (11")

Parrot green silk dupion

construction

All seam allowances are 13mm (½").

○ right side of fabric   ◐ interlining

1. Preparing the embroidered linen

Remove any remaining tacking. Place the embroidered linen, face down, onto a soft, padded surface and press with a warm, dry iron, squaring the corners and straightening edges.

2. Making templates

Make a photocopy of each stitched piece. Cut out the photocopy of each piece just inside the outer edge of the Celtic cross stitch or back stitch border. These will be used as templates for cutting the interfacings and interlining.

3. Preparing the lightweight fusible interfacing

Using the templates, cut and label pieces of lightweight interfacing to fit inside the outer edge of the Celtic cross stitch or back stitch border of each panel.

4. Preparing the medium weight fusible interfacing

Using the templates cut and label pieces of medium weight interfacing to fit inside the outer edge of the Celtic cross stitch border for the etui base and sides and waxer box base and sides using the ruler and craft knife.

NOTE *The medium weight interfacing for the needlebook front and back is cut after the interlining has been attached to the linen panels and the seam allowances have been secured.*

5. Applying the lightweight interfacing and cutting out the linen and silk

Position the pieces of lightweight interfacing, adhesive side down, over the wrong side of the stitched panels, checking to ensure that the interfacing sits just inside the outer edge of the Celtic cross stitch borders or the back stitch outlines. Fuse in place. Cut out each piece, leaving a 13mm (½") seam allowance from the outer edge of the Celtic cross stitch borders and the back stitch outlines. Using the linen pieces as templates, cut pieces of silk for the etui base

and sides, needlebook covers, and waxer box base and sides.

6. Preparing the interlining

Use the ruler and craft knife to cut out the interlining and label each piece. Using the templates, cut pieces of interlining for the etui base and sides, needlebook covers, waxer box base and sides, pincushion base and scissor fob panels.

7. Cords and tassels

Etui: using six, 105cm (41") lengths of **A** make a 35cm (14") twisted cord. At the centre of the cord apply a dab of craft glue and allow to dry. Cut the cord in half at the glued point.

Needlebook: using three, 105cm (41") lengths of **A** make a 35cm (14") twisted cord. At the centre of the cord apply a dab of craft glue and allow to dry. Cut the cord in half at the glued point.

Waxer box: using four, 105cm (41") lengths of **A** make a 35cm (14") twisted cord. At the centre of the cord apply a dab of craft glue and allow to dry. Cut the cord in half at the glued point.

Scissor fob: using six, 120cm (47") lengths of **A** make a 40cm (16") twisted cord. Using three, 60cm (24") lengths of **A** make a 20cm (8") twisted cord for the tassel neck. Bind the knotted end of the 40cm (16") cord to secure and trim away the knots. Bring the bound and looped ends of the cord together and stitch securely (diag 1).

To make the tassel, wrap the piece of firm card with **A** until the skirt is the desired fullness. Cut the thread bundle at the base. Take one end of the bundle over the joined ends of the twisted cord (diag 2). Referring to the step-by-step instructions on page 107, wrap the 20cm (8") cord around the thread bundle to form the tassel neck. Trim the base of the skirt so that it is even.

Stitch the base and side panels together following the instructions and referring to the diagram (diag 5).

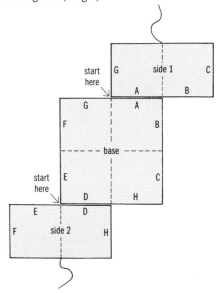

8. ETUI

Preparing the etui

The base and side panels are constructed in the same manner. Mitre the corners and finger press the seam allowance to the wrong side, folding on the first linen thread outside the Celtic cross stitch border. Press with a dry iron. Open out the folds and centre the interlining over the wrong side of the linen. Refold the seam allowance and stitch the mitres. Lace the seam allowance to keep the interlining in place (diag 3).

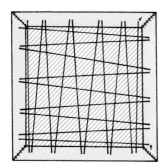

Repeat for the side panels.

Centre the medium weight interfacing, adhesive side down, over the wrong side of the base silk lining piece and fuse in place. Mitre the corners and fold in the seam allowance. Press the corners and edges and stitch the mitres. Repeat for the side panels.

Constructing the etui

Place the linen base panel, wrong side uppermost, on a flat surface. With wrong sides together, centre the silk lining over the linen and pin together. Stitch the silk lining to the linen with slip stitch along each edge using the dusky pink beading thread.

Stitch the lengths of twisted cord securely to the seam allowance at the centre of the side panels, stitching one adjacent to the zigzag border and the other adjacent to the diamond and star border (diag 4).

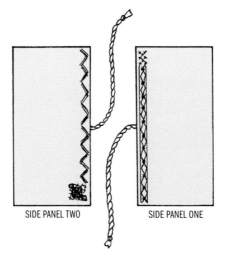

SIDE PANEL TWO   SIDE PANEL ONE

Attach the lining to the linen on the side panels in the same manner as the base.

Place the etui base, wrong side uppermost, on a flat surface. Place side panel 1, wrong side uppermost, adjacent to the base panel so that the A edges are aligned.

Using joining stitch and **A**, stitch the panels together along the A edges, beginning at the centre of the base panel. When reaching the corner, gently bend the side panel around and stitch the B edges together.

Gently bend the base panel up and stitch the C edges together. Repeat with side panel 2, beginning with the D edges and continuing with the E then F edges. Bring the G edges together and stitch then the H edges.

9. NEEDLEBOOK

Preparing the needlebook

Prepare the linen and interlining in the same manner as the etui.

*Measure the finished linen panels and cut the medium weight fusible interfacing to this measurement.

Prepare the silk lining and medium weight interfacing in the same manner as the etui.

Stitch each length of twisted cord to the seam allowance at the centre point on one side of each cover, taking care to ensure that the back cover will be correctly aligned when the book is closed (diag 6).

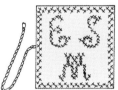

Constructing the needlebook

With wrong sides together, centre one silk lining over one linen panel and pin. Stitch the silk lining to the linen with slip stitch along each edge using the dusky pink beading thread. Repeat with the second panel and lining.

Cut two pieces of green wool felt slightly smaller than the silk lining pieces. Position one piece of felt over each silk lining panel, aligning one edge of the felt with the spine edge of the silk and stitch in place using the beading thread.

To make the spine, place the two covers together, linen side outermost, and hold in place with an elastic band so that the aligned edges where the felt pages have been attached are accessible. These are the two edges that will be joined. Press the length of **T**. Thread each end of the ribbon into a tapestry needle. Beginning at the upper edge on one side, take one end of the ribbon through the first back stitch on the back cover and the other end through the first back stitch on the front cover (diag 7).

Take care to ensure that the ribbon is centred and remains flat. Working in the same manner as lacing up shoes, cross the ribbons and take them through every back stitch on the opposite side. Continue working in this manner to the end. After threading the ribbons through the last back stitch on each side, remove the needles and tie the ribbon tails into a bow. Trim away any excess ribbon and cut the ends at a 45 degree angle.

10. WAXER BOX

Prepare and construct the waxer box in the same manner as the etui.

11. PINCUSHION

Preparing the pincushion

Prepare the base of the pincushion in the same manner as the etui base. Mitre the corners and fold in the seam allowance on the side panels. Stitch the mitres and press.

Constructing the pincushion

Construct the pincushion in the same manner as the etui. Fill with fibre-fill and stitch the top opening closed with joining stitch using **A**. Attach the jade bead at the centre top using the dusky pink beading thread.

12. SCISSOR FOB

Preparing the scissor fob

Mitre the corners and fold in the seam allowance on each side of each panel. Open out the folds and centre the interlining over the wrong side of the linen. Refold the seam allowance. Stitch the mitres and press.

Constructing the scissor fob

With wrong sides facing and using **A**, stitch the panels together with joining stitch from A to B (diag 8).

Open the panels and place the cord, tassel side down, between them. Close the panels and continue stitching from C to D, taking care not to catch the cords as this will prevent them from sliding. Attach the looped end of the cord to a pair of embroidery scissors.

CONSTRUCTION

good for the goose box

For colour photos and full details see pages 60–69.

construction

All seam allowances are 13mm (½") unless otherwise specified.

 right side of fabric interfacing interlining

1. Preparing the embroidered linen

Remove any remaining tacking. Place the embroidered linen, face down, onto a soft, padded surface and press with a warm, dry iron, squaring the corners and straightening edges.

2. Making templates

Make two photocopies of each stitched side panel. Cut out one photocopy of each piece along the inside edge of the three-sided stitch border. These will be used for cutting interfacing. Cut out the second copies just inside the outer edge of the three-sided stitch border. These will be used as templates for cutting interlining.

3. Preparing the lightweight fusible interfacing

Using the smaller photocopy templates, cut pieces of lightweight interfacing to fit inside the three-sided stitch border of each stitched panel. Using the triangle templates, cut interfacing for the lid and base.

4. Applying the lightweight interfacing and cutting out the linen and silk lining

Centre the pieces of lightweight interfacing, adhesive side down, over the wrong side of the stitched panels, checking to ensure that the interfacing sits inside the three-sided stitch outlines (diag 1).

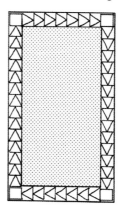

Fuse in place. Centre the interfacing over the back of the lid and base panels and fuse in place.

Cut out each linen piece leaving a 13mm (½") seam allowance from the outline. On the base and lid pieces, cut out 13mm (½") from the edge of the interfacing. Using the linen pieces as templates, cut pieces of silk lining for the side panels, lid and base.

5. Preparing the interlining

Use the ruler and craft knife to cut out the interlining and label each piece.

Using the larger photocopy templates cut two pieces of interlining for each side panel. On one piece for each panel, trim away 1mm-2mm (¹⁄₁₆") along each side and label. These will be used for the lining. Using the triangle templates, cut two pieces of interlining each for the lid and base. Trim one piece for the base triangle and label in

the same manner as the side panels. This will be used for the base lining.

6. Cords

Using four, 60cm (24") lengths of **A**, make a 15cm (6") twisted cord.

7. Preparing the panels, lid and base

On each linen side panel, mitre the corners, fold in the seam allowance on the first linen thread outside the three-sided stitch border and press. Open out the seams and position the interlining inside. Refold the corners and seams. Stitch the mitres. Lace the seam allowances using **A**. Prepare the silk lining pieces in a similar manner but do not fold in the seam allowance on the lower edge of each lining panel (diag 2).

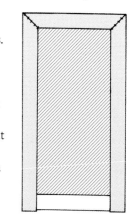

When lacing the lining panels, take small stitches just below the edge of the interlining on the lower edge (diag 3).

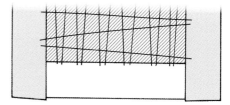

Prepare the lid, base and linings in the same manner, trimming the seam allowances as required.

8. Assembling the panels

With wrong sides together and matching the top edges, stitch one lining piece to one linen panel with joining stitch, using the yellow beading thread, along the top edge only. Repeat for the remaining panels.

Using joining stitch and **A**, stitch two panels together down one long edge. Join the third panel to the remaining edge of the second panel then join the remaining edge of the third panel to the first panel in the same manner to form a triangle. The seam allowances of the silk lining pieces should protrude at the base (diag 4).

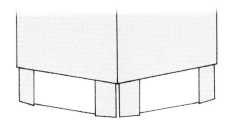

9. Assembling the lid and base

With wrong sides together and matching edges, stitch the lid and lid lining together around the outer edge with joining stitch using the yellow beading thread. As there are no three-sided stitches to use as a guide, make the stitches as even as possible, adding an **M** bead before working each vertical stitch.

10. Constructing the etui

Position the linen base over the base of the etui, ensuring that the lining seam allowances are tucked inside, and stitch in place with joining stitch using **A**.

Push the base lining firmly down into the etui, smoothing the sides and trapping the loose seam allowances.

Measure in approximately 13mm (½") from the upper corner on each side of the back of the etui and attach an **L** bead at the upper edge using the yellow beading thread (diag 5).

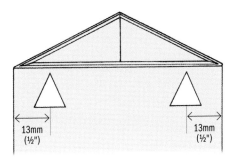

13mm (½")   13mm (½")

Take care to ensure that the base panel is correctly aligned. To make the hinges, centre the lid at the top of the etui, taking care to ensure that the embroidery is correctly aligned and mark the positions where the beads on the lid edge align with the top of the **L** beads. Thread the looped end of the twisted cord through a large needle. Carefully take the needle behind one of the marked lid beads and pull the cord through, leaving a 5cm (2") tail. Bind the centre of the cord with tape and cut in half. Take the remaining half of the cord behind the second marked lid bead (diag 6).

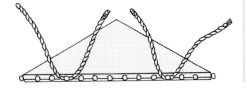

Remove the needle and tie each half of the cord around the **L** bead. Trim the cord ends to the required length and knot each one firmly. Stitch the remaining **L** bead to the upper edge of the front corner using the yellow beading thread. Using **A**, work a Hedebo stitch loop at the front corner of the lid to correspond.

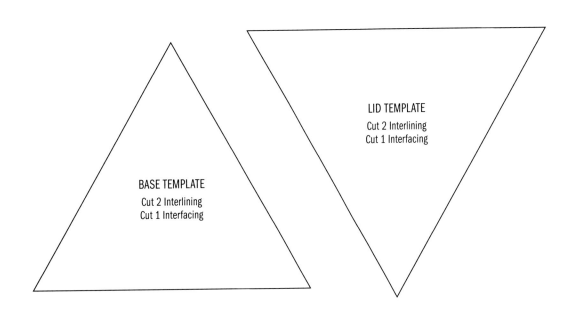

BASE TEMPLATE
Cut 2 Interlining
Cut 1 Interfacing

LID TEMPLATE
Cut 2 Interlining
Cut 1 Interfacing

cardinal pocket

For colour photos and full details see pages 70–75.

construction

All seam allowances are 13mm (½") unless specified.

 right side of fabric   interfacing

1. Preparing the embroidered linen

Remove any remaining tacking. Place the embroidered linen, face down, onto a soft, padded surface and press with a warm, dry iron, squaring the corners and straightening edges.

2. Making templates

Make a photocopy of each stitched piece. Label and cut out the photocopy of each piece just inside the back stitch outline using the ruler and craft knife. The pocket template should be cut into three pieces, one each for the front, spine and back, cutting each side of the internal back stitch lines on each panel (diag 1).

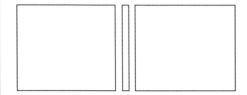

These will be used as templates for cutting interfacing and board.

3. Preparing the lightweight fusible interfacing

Using the templates, cut pieces of lightweight interfacing to fit inside the back stitch border of each panel.

4. Applying the lightweight interfacing and cutting out the linen

Position the pieces of interfacing, adhesive side down, over the wrong side of the panels. Check to ensure that the interfacing sits just inside the back stitch outline. Fuse in place.

Cut out the linen pocket and scissor fob panels, leaving a 13mm (½") seam allowance from the outline.

5. Preparing the comic board

Using the photocopy templates, ruler and craft knife, cut and label a piece of comic board to fit the front and back of the pocket and scissor fob panels, checking to ensure that each piece fits inside the back stitch outlines.

6. Preparing the medium weight fusible interfacing

Using the photocopy templates cut pieces of medium weight interfacing to fit the front and back pocket panels.

7. Cords and tassel

Pocket: using six, 130cm (51") lengths of **A**, make a 43cm (17") twisted cord.

Scissor fob: using six, 100cm (40") lengths of **A**, make a 33cm (13") twisted cord. Bind

the knotted end of the cord securely with matching thread and trim away the knots. Bring both ends of the cord together and stitch securely (diag 2).

Using four, 75cm (30") lengths of **A**, make a 25cm (10") twisted cord for the tassel neck.

To make the tassel, wrap the piece of firm card with **A** until the skirt is the desired fullness. Cut the thread bundle at the base. Take one end of the bundle over the joined ends of the twisted cord (diag 3).

Referring to the step-by-step instructions on page 107, wrap the small cord around the thread bundle to form the tassel neck. Trim the base of the skirt so that it is even.

8. POCKET

Preparing the linen panel

Work a Hedebo stitch loop at each side of the upper edge of the front panel, working over the second and third back stitches from each side and using **A**. Each loop should be large enough for a twisted cord to pass through (diag 4).

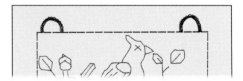

Position each comic board panel over the back of the respective embroidered panel and lace in place using the beading thread, taking each stitch under the back stitch lines on each side (diag 5).

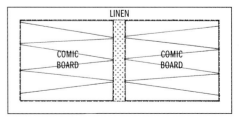

Mitre the corners of the linen and finger press and finger press. Press the corners with a dry iron. Fold in the seam allowance on each side, folding on the first linen thread outside the back stitch border. Finger press the seams then press with a dry iron. Stitch the mitres and lace the seam allowances along the long edges only (diag 6).

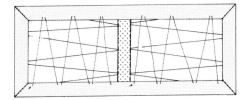

Preparing the lining and internal pockets

Measure the length of the stitched area of the entire pocket and add 24.5cm (9⅝"). This is the measurement for the long sides of the silk lining. Measuring from one short end and using the heat-soluble fabric marker, mark this distance along each long side of the silk rectangle. Rule a line across the silk at this point and trim away the excess fabric.

Measure the width of the stitched pocket panel and add 2.5cm (1"). This is the measurement for the short sides of the silk lining. Working from one long edge, measure and mark this distance along the silk rectangle and trim away the excess (diag 7).

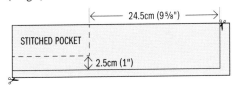

Remove any visible marker with a hair dryer.

Place the silk rectangle on a flat surface right side uppermost. To make the first pocket, measure in 8.3cm (3¼") from the left-hand short edge. At this point fold the fabric over and press (diag 8).

Turn to the wrong side, with the fold at the right-hand side. Measure in 5.5cm (2³⁄₁₆") from the first fold and fold the left-hand end of the fabric to the right side (diag 9).

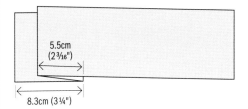

Repeat the folding process at the opposite short end of the silk rectangle to make a second pocket.

Place the folded silk rectangle on a flat surface wrong side uppermost. Centre the two pieces of medium weight interfacing over the silk. Move the pieces of interfacing apart, towards the short edges of the silk, until there is 6mm (¼") between them. This should match the placement of the comic board panels on the wrong side of the linen pocket panels. Fuse the medium weight interfacing pieces to the silk.

Turn the silk to the right side. If desired, using sewing thread, work tiny running stitch along the centre of one pocket, reinforcing with extra stitches at each end (diag 10).

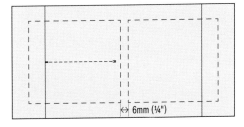

Mitre the corners of the silk lining and fold in the seam allowance. Press the corners and edges and stitch the mitres.

Attaching the needle page

Trim the piece of gold wool felt to measure 4.5cm x 5.5cm wide (1¾" x 2⅛"). Position over the undivided silk pocket so that one long edge is 5mm (³⁄₁₆") away from the folded edge of the pocket. Using the beading thread and the buttons, attach two corners of the felt to the pocket, taking care to only stitch through the first two layers of silk, keeping the pocket open (diag 11).

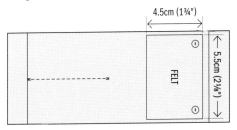

Constructing the pocket

With wrong sides together, position the silk lining over the linen panel. The lining should be slightly smaller than the linen piece. Pin in place. Using ladder stitch and the beading thread, and beginning at the upper corner for the back panel, ladder stitch the lining to the linen pocket piece around three sides, working along the first long end, the short end with the Hedebo stitch loops, and along the remaining long end.

Begin to ladder stitch the remaining short side closed, as far as the second back stitch. Insert 13mm (½") of one end of the twisted cord into the seam opening and position

over the linen seam allowance between the second and third back stitches. Stitch the cord securely to the linen seam allowance, stitching back and forth through the cord and seam allowance a few times. Take the remaining end of the cord and thread it through the corresponding Hedebo stitch loop, from inside to outside, and through the second loop from outside to inside. Bring the cord back to the open seam and stitch 13mm (½") of the end of the cord to the linen seam allowance at the mirror position to the first end (diag 12).

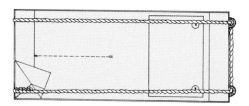

Ladder stitch the remaining seam closed.

To close the stitching pocket, pull the twisted cord upwards.

9. SCISSOR FOB

Preparing the scissor fob

On each linen piece mitre the corners, fold in the seam allowance and press. Open out the seams and position the board inside. Refold the corners and seams. Trim the seam allowance if necessary and stitch the mitres. Press.

Constructing the scissor fob

Using **A** and with wrong sides together and matching edges, stitch the fob pieces together with joining stitch between A and B (diag 13).

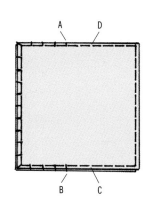

Open the panels and place the cord, tassel end down, between them. Close the panels and continue stitching from C to D, taking care not to catch the cord as this will prevent it from sliding. Attach the looped end of the cord to a small pair of embroidery scissors.

mermaid bag etui

For colour photos and full details see pages 76–85.

cutting out

Where pattern pieces are not provided, cut the pieces according to the measurements below.

Sea-theme blue and white print cotton

Bag lining: cut one 23cm x 25cm wide (9" x 10")

construction

All seam allowances are 13mm (½").

 right side of fabric   interfacing

1. Preparing the embroidered linen

Place the embroidered linen, face down, onto a soft, padded surface and press with a warm, dry iron, squaring the corners and straightening edges.

2. Making templates

Make a photocopy of each stitched piece with a stitched border. Cut each photocopy just inside the outer edge of the Celtic cross stitch or inside the back stitch border. These will be used as templates for cutting interfacing and interlining.

3. Preparing the lightweight and medium weight fusible interfacing

Using the photocopy templates, cut pieces of lightweight fusible interfacing to fit inside the back stitch border of the scissor fob panels. Using the bag base/orts pot inner base oval template cut two pieces of lightweight fusible interfacing.

Using the photocopies of the bag side panel and orts pot side panel, cut one piece of medium weight fusible interfacing for the bag panel and two for the orts pot panel.

4. Applying the interfacing and cutting out the linen and cotton lining

Position the pieces of lightweight interfacing, adhesive side down, over the wrong side of the scissor fob panels, checking to ensure that the interfacing sits just inside the back stitch outlines. Fuse in place. Centre one interfacing oval over the wrong side of the bag base embroidery and one interfacing oval over the wrong side of the orts pot inner base embroidery and fuse in place.

Position the piece of medium weight fusible interfacing, adhesive side down, over the wrong side of the bag side panel and the piece of medium weight interfacing over the orts pot side panel and fuse in place. *Using **B**, work a diamond eyelet over twelve threads at each marked position between the upper borders on the bag side panel. Using the dressmaker's awl, open up the centre of each eyelet so that the hole is large enough to accommodate the twisted cord.

Cut out the linen scissor fob, bag side panel and orts pot side panel leaving a 13mm (½") seam allowance from the outline. Cut out the bag base and orts pot inner base leaving a 13mm (½") seam allowance from the edge of the interfacing oval. Using the linen oval base as a template, cut an oval from the blue and white wavy print cotton.

Using the orts pot linen side panel as a template, cut a piece of blue and white wavy print cotton for the orts pot lining. Centre the second piece of medium weight fusible interfacing over the wrong side of the cotton print and fuse in place.

5. Preparing the interlining

Use sharp scissors or the ruler and craft knife to cut out the interlining and label each piece.

Using the photocopy templates, cut pieces of interlining to fit just inside the back stitch border of each scissor fob panel. Using the bag base/orts pot inner base oval template cut three from the interlining. Using the orts pot base oval template, cut one of interlining.

6. Cords and tassels

Etui: using three, 105cm (42") lengths of **A** and **B**, make a 35cm (14") two-colour twisted cord. Using three, 60cm (24") lengths of **A**, make a 20cm (8") twisted cord for the tassel neck. *Once the two-colour cord has been taken through the eyelets at the top of the bag, bind the knotted end of the cord securely with matching thread and trim away the knots (diag 1).

Bring both ends of the cord together and stitch securely (diag 2).

To make the tassel, wrap the piece of firm card with **B** until the skirt is the desired fullness. Cut the thread bundle at the base. Take one end of the bundle over the joined ends of the twisted cord (diag 3). Referring to the step-by-step instructions on page 107, wrap the small cord around the thread bundle to form the tassel neck. Trim the base of the skirt so that it is even.

Scissor fob: using four, 90cm (36") lengths of **B**, make a 30cm (12") twisted cord. Bind the knotted end of the cord securely with matching thread and trim away the knots.

Bring both ends of the cord together and stitch securely.

To make the tassel, wrap the piece of firm card with **B** until the skirt is the desired fullness. Cut the thread bundle at the base. Take one end of the bundle over the joined ends of the twisted cord. Wrap the thread bundle with a length of **A** to form the tassel neck. Trim the base of the skirt so that it is even.

7. ETUI

Preparing the linen

At the lower edge of the bag side panel, fold the seam allowance to the back, folding on the first linen thread outside the Celtic cross stitch border. Repeat on each side edge, mitre the lower corners and fold on the first linen thread outside the tacked line. Finger press.

Leaving a tail at each end, work a line of gathering 6mm (¼") in from the raw edge on the bag base. Centre one interlining oval over the interfacing on the wrong side of the fabric, pull up the gathering threads and tie off firmly. Press. Mark the centre of one long side of the oval with a pin.

Preparing the lining

On the upper edge of the rectangle of sea-theme print cotton, fold 13mm (½") to the wrong side and press. Measure down 10.5cm (4¼") from the folded edge and mark with a pin. At this point, fold the lower section of the fabric up, ensuring that the right sides are together, remove the pin and press (diag 4).

Measure down 6.5cm (2½") from the raw edge and mark with a pin. Fold the fabric down at this point, remove the pin and press to form the pocket (diag 5).

Measure in 7cm (2¾") from the left-hand side and mark with a pin. Repeat on the right-hand side. Measure the distance between the two pins and mark the centre point with a pin. Using a removable fabric marker, rule a line down the pocket section at each marked point. Using the white sewing thread, work a line of back stitch or running stitch along each line, working several reinforcing stitches at each end (diag 6).

Fold under the seam allowance on each side edge of the lining and press, taking care to ensure that it is approximately the same width as the linen panel.

At the upper edge of the linen panel, fold the fabric to the wrong side at the halfway point between the two rows of eyelets. The eyelets should line up. Press the upper edge carefully. With wrong sides together and matching the upper edge of the lining with the edge of the Celtic cross stitch border, slip stitch the lining in place along the upper edge (diag 7).

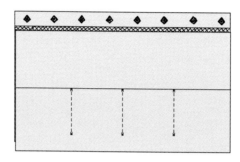

diag 7

Leaving a tail at each end, work a line of gathering 6mm (¼") in from the raw edge on the print cotton oval cut for the bag lining base. Centre one interlining oval over the wrong side of the fabric, pull up the gathering threads and tie off firmly. Press.

Constructing the etui

Position one lower corner of the linen panel at the marked centre point of the linen base oval (diag 8).

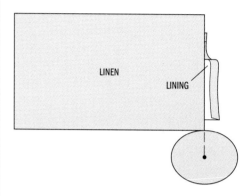

diag 8

Beginning at this point, stitch the base to the lower edge of the bag side panel using ladder stitch and the blue sewing thread. Open the lining out. With right sides together and matching edges, stitch the side seam of the linen and lining. Press the seam open (diag 9).

Turn to the right side. Attach the charms and buttons using the white sewing thread.

Push the lining down inside the bag. Taking care not to catch the pockets, push the base lining down into the bag. *Beginning at the centre front, thread the two-colour twisted cord through the eyelets around the bag. Once the tassel is complete, stitch the mermaid charm to the tassel neck.

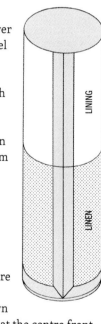

diag 9

....

8. ORTS POT

Preparing the linen

Mitre the corners and fold the seam allowance to the back on each side of the

diag 4

diag 5

diag 6

linen, folding on the first thread outside the stitched or tacked border and finger press. Leaving a tail at each end, work a line of gathering 6mm (¼") in from the raw edge on the inner base linen. Centre the remaining smaller interlining oval over the interfacing on the wrong side of the fabric, pull up the gathering threads and tie off firmly. Press.

Preparing the lining

Fold the seam allowance to the back along the upper and side edges and press. With wrong sides together and matching the upper folded edges, stitch the lining to the linen with joining stitch using the blue sewing thread.

Leaving a tail at each end, work a line of gathering 6mm (¼") in from the raw edge on the print cotton oval cut for the orts pot base. Centre the interlining oval over the wrong side of the fabric, pull up the gathering threads and tie off firmly. Press. Mark the centre of one long side of the oval with a pin.

Constructing the orts pot

Stitch the print cotton base to the linen and stitch the linen and lining side seam in the same manner as the bag. Turn to the right side. Attach the coral and button using the white sewing thread. Push the lining down inside the pot. Push the linen base lining down into the pot.

Carefully push the bag down into the orts pot. The upper edge of the pot should align with the lower edge of the waves on the bag.

....

9. SCISSOR FOB

Preparing the scissor fob

On each linen piece mitre the corners, fold in the seam allowance and press. Open out the seams and position the interlining inside. Refold the corners and seams. Trim the seam allowance if necessary and stitch the mitres. Press.

Constructing the scissor fob

With wrong sides together and matching

edges, stitch the fob pieces together with joining stitch between A and B using **A** and working a stitch every two border stitches (diag 10).

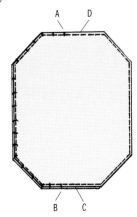

Open the panels and place the cord, tassel end down, between them. Close the panels and continue stitching from C to D, taking care not to catch the cord as this will prevent it from sliding. Attach the looped end of the cord to a pair of embroidery scissors.

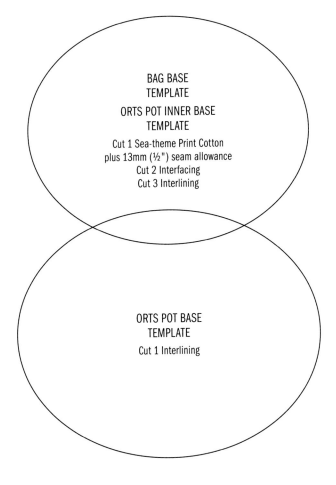

BAG BASE
TEMPLATE

ORTS POT INNER BASE
TEMPLATE

Cut 1 Sea-theme Print Cotton
plus 13mm (½") seam allowance
Cut 2 Interfacing
Cut 3 Interlining

ORTS POT BASE
TEMPLATE

Cut 1 Interlining

CONSTRUCTION

tasmanian needle tidy

For colour photos and full details see pages 86–95.

construction

All seam allowances are 13mm (½").

 right side of fabric   interfacing   interlining

1. Preparing the embroidered linen

Remove any remaining tacking. Place the embroidered linen, face down, onto a soft, padded surface and press with a warm, dry iron, squaring the corners and straightening edges.

2. Making templates

Make a photocopy of each stitched piece. Label and cut out the photocopy of each piece just inside the back stitch outlines of each panel. Discard the pieces for the fold panels.

These will be used as templates for cutting interfacing and interlining.

3. Preparing the lightweight fusible interfacing

Using the templates, cut pieces of lightweight interfacing to fit inside the back stitch border of each stitched panel. The fold panels are not interfaced.

4. Preparing the medium weight fusible interfacing

Using the templates cut and label pieces of medium weight interfacing to fit inside the outer edge of the back stitch border for each tidy panel and the pocket panel.

5. Preparing the interlining

Using the photocopy templates, ruler and craft knife, cut and label a piece of interlining to fit each stitched panel, checking to ensure that each piece fits inside the back stitch outlines.

6. Applying the lightweight interfacing and cutting out the linen and silk

Position the pieces of interfacing, adhesive side down, over the wrong side of the stitched panels. Check to ensure that the interfacing sits just inside the back stitch outlines. Fuse in place.

Cut out the needle tidy panels as one piece and the pocket and scissor fob panels, leaving a 13mm (½") seam allowance from the back stitch outlines.

Using the linen pieces as templates, cut pieces of silk for the needle tidy and pocket.

7. Cords and tassel

Tidy: using six, 90cm (36") lengths of **A**, make a 30cm (12") twisted cord. Apply a dab of craft glue just inside the loop and the knot at the ends of the cord, work the glue into the cord, tightening the twist, and allow to dry. Cutting at an angle, trim each end of the cord at the glued point.

Using four, 45cm (18") lengths of **A**, make a 15cm (6") twisted cord.

Scissor fob: using six, 105cm (42") lengths of **A**, make a 35cm (14") twisted cord. Bind the knotted end of the cord securely with matching thread and trim away the knots. Bring both ends of the cord together and stitch securely (diag 1).

Using four, 60cm (24") lengths of **A**, make a 20cm (8") twisted cord for the tassel neck.

To make the tassel, wrap the piece of firm card with **A** until the skirt is the desired fullness. Cut the thread bundle at the base. Take one end of the bundle over the joined ends of the twisted cord (diag 2).

Referring to the step-by-step instructions on page 107, wrap the small cord around the thread bundle to form the tassel neck. Trim the base of the skirt so that it is even.

8. NEEDLE TIDY

Preparing the linen panels

Centre the button over the stem of the centre banskia flower and stitch in place using **D**.

Position each interlining piece over the back of the respective embroidered panel and lace in place using the sewing thread, taking each stitch under the back stitch lines on each side (diag 3).

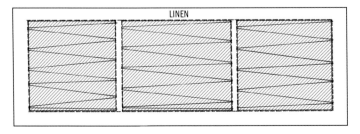

LINEN

diag 3

Using the dressmaker's awl, open up the eyelets in the front flap fold panel. Thread one end of the 30cm (12") cord from front to back through one eyelet. Knot the end of the cord behind the panel and stitch the tail to the interlining using the sewing thread. Repeat at the remaining eyelet with the remaining end of the cord.

Mitre the corners of the linen and finger press. Press the corners with a dry iron. Fold in the seam allowance on each side, folding on the first linen thread outside the back stitch border. Finger press the seams then press with a dry iron. Stitch the mitres and lace the seam allowances along the long edges only (diag 4).

Preparing the pocket

Centre the piece of medium weight fusible interfacing for the pocket over the wrong side of the silk pocket lining piece and fuse in place.

Using the sewing thread and leaving a tail, work a line of gathering 6mm (¼") in from the curved edge of the linen and silk (diag 5).

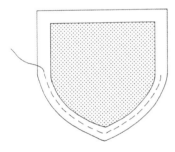

Position the pocket interlining on the wrong side of the linen pocket. Pull up the gathering stitches, evenly distributing the gathers around the curve. Tie off the gathering thread and press. Remove the interlining and repeat for the silk lining. Remove the interlining from the silk lining and discard.

On the linen pocket, mitre the corners, fold in the remaining seam allowances and press. Stitch the mitres. Repeat with the silk lining, checking that it is a little smaller than the linen pocket.

With wrong sides together and upper edges aligned, centre the silk lining over the linen pocket. Ladder stitch the silk to the linen using the sewing thread.

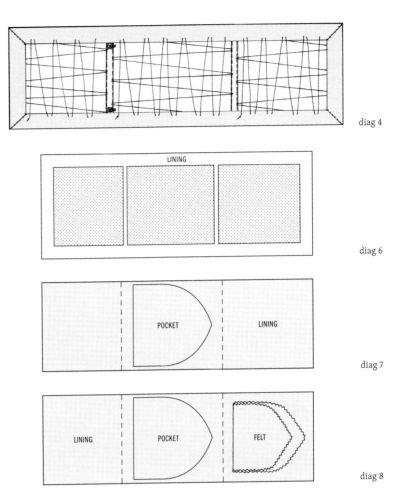

diag 4

diag 6

diag 7

diag 8

Preparing the needle tidy lining

Place the silk rectangle for the lining on a flat surface with the wrong side uppermost. Centre the pieces of medium weight interfacing for the front flap, back and inner front flap, spacing them 3mm (⅛") apart and ensuring they are aligned (diag 6).

Fuse in place.

Mitre the corners of the silk lining and fold in the seam allowance. Press the corners and edges and stitch the mitres.

With silk linings facing together, centre the prepared pocket over the back panel of the lining, with the opening facing the front flap area (diag 7).

Leaving the upper edge open, stitch the pocket to the lining with joining stitch using the sewing thread.

Using the black pen, trace the needlepage template and foldline marking onto tracing paper. Pin or tape the tracing to the violet wool felt and cut out using the scallop pinking shears. Using the tracing as a guide, fold the felt at the indicated line and press. Centre the folded pages over the inner flap of the lining, orientated to correspond with the pocket (diag 8).

Pin the lower page to the lining. Lift the upper page and stitch the felt to the lining along the foldline with running stitch using the sewing thread, working reinforcing stitches at each end. Remove the pins.

Constructing the needle tidy

Stitch 13mm (½") of the 15cm (6") twisted cord to the seam allowance at the upper edge of the front flap panel using the sewing thread.

With wrong sides together, position the silk lining over the prepared linen panel, ensuring the needlepage section is behind the inside front flap. The lining should be slightly smaller than the linen. Pin in place. Using the sewing thread, ladder stitch the lining to the linen. Fold the inside front flap up over the pocket and the front flap down over the inside front flap. Wind the short cord around the button to hold the tidy closed.

....

9. SCISSOR FOB

Preparing the scissor fob

On each linen piece mitre the corners, fold in the seam allowance and press. Open out the seams and position the interlining inside. Refold the corners and seams. Trim the seam allowance if necessary and stitch the mitres. Press.

Constructing the scissor fob

Using **A** and with wrong sides together and matching edges, stitch the panels together with joining stitch between A and B (diag 9).

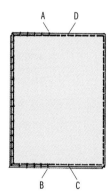

Open the panels and place the cord, tassel end down, between them. Close the panels and continue stitching from C to D, taking care not to catch the cord as this will prevent it from sliding. Attach the looped end of the cord to a pair of embroidery scissors.

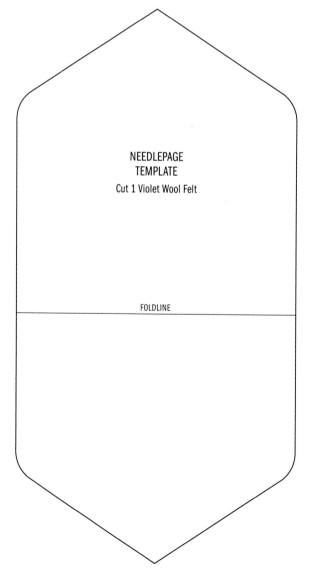

NEEDLEPAGE
TEMPLATE

Cut 1 Violet Wool Felt

FOLDLINE

holbein hexagon etui

For colour photos and full details see pages 96–105.

cutting out

Where pattern pieces are not provided, cut the pieces according to the measurements below.

Antique blue silk dupion

Pincushion lid: cut one, 9.5cm x 33cm wide (3¾" x 13")

Cutting layout

Antique blue silk dupion

1. Etui side panel lining (6)
2. Etui lid lining
3. Etui pincushion lid
4. Etui pincushion circle
5. Needlebook lining (2)
6. Scissor sheath lining (2)

50cm (20")

40cm (16")

construction

All seam allowances are 13mm (½") unless otherwise specified.

 right side of fabric   interlining

1. Preparing the embroidered linen

Remove any remaining tacking. Place the embroidered linen, face down, onto a soft, padded surface and press with a warm, dry iron, squaring the corners and straightening edges.

2. Making templates

Make a photocopy of each piece with a stitched border and two copies of the needlebook covers. Cut out one photocopy of each piece just inside the back stitch border. Cut out the second copies of the needlebook covers just outside the back stitch border. These will be used as templates for cutting interfacing, interlining and board.

3. Preparing the lightweight fusible interfacing

Using the photocopy templates, cut pieces of lightweight interfacing to fit inside the back stitch border of each stitched panel. Using the hexagon templates, cut a piece of lightweight interfacing for the base and inner base.

4. Applying the lightweight interfacing and cutting out the linen and silk lining

Position the pieces of lightweight interfacing, adhesive side down, over the wrong side of the stitched panels, checking to ensure that the interfacing sits just inside the back stitch outlines. Fuse in place. Centre the hexagons of interfacing, adhesive side down, over the wrong side of the base and inner base embroidery. Fuse in place.

Cut out each linen piece leaving a 13mm (½") seam allowance from the outline or interfacing edges. Using the linen pieces as templates, cut a piece of silk lining for the etui side panels, needlebook and scissor sheath front and back. Using the lid template, cut out a silk hexagon, adding a 13mm (½") seam allowance at each side. Cut a circle of silk using the circle template.

5. Preparing the comic board and interlining

Use the ruler and craft knife to cut out the comic board and interlining and label each piece.

Using the photocopy templates, cut pieces of comic board to fit just inside the back stitch border of each etui side panel. Using the etui lid and base hexagon templates, cut one each of comic board.

Using the photocopy templates cut a piece of interlining for each of the etui side panels, needlebook, scissor sheath and scissor fob front and back. Using the second photocopy templates, cut two pieces of interlining for the needlebook lining. Using the scissor sheath template, cut one piece of interlining.

6. Preparing the medium weight interfacing

Using the scissor sheath template, cut two pieces of medium weight interfacing.

7. Cords and tassels

Etui: using two, 38cm (15") lengths of **A** and **B**, make a 12.5cm (5") two-colour twisted cord. Bind the knotted end of the cord securely with matching thread and trim away the knots. Bring both ends of the cord together and stitch securely (diag 1).

Using two, 60cm (24") lengths of **A** and **B**, make a 20cm (8") two-colour twisted cord for the tassel neck.

To make the tassel, wrap the piece of firm card with **A** until the skirt is the desired fullness. Cut the thread bundle at the base. Take one end of the bundle over the joined ends of the twisted cord (diag 2).

Referring to the step-by-step instructions on page 107, wrap the small cord around the thread bundle to form the tassel neck. Trim the base of the skirt so that it is even.

Scissor fob: using three, 1m (39") lengths of **A** and **B**, make a 33cm (13") two-colour twisted cord. Make a tassel cord in the same manner as before. Using two, 60cm (24") lengths of **A** and **B**, make a 20cm (8") two-colour twisted cord for the tassel neck. Using **A**, make a tassel in the same manner as before.

. . . .

8. ETUI

Preparing the linen panels

Position each comic board panel over the back of the respective embroidered side panel and lace in place using the beading thread, taking each stitch under the back stitch lines on each side (diag 3).

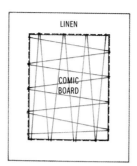

Mitre the corners of the linen and finger press. Press the corners with a dry iron. Fold in the seam allowance on each side, folding on the first linen thread outside the back stitch border.

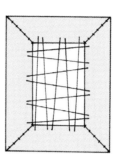

Finger press the seams then press with a dry iron. Stitch the mitres and lace the seam allowances (diag 4).

Centre the hexagon board for the base over the wrong side of the embroidered linen. Fold in each seam allowance in turn, working two tacking stitches to hold each corner, and lace the seam allowances (diag 5).

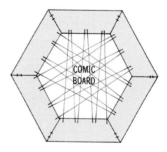

Repeat for the inner base board and linen.

Preparing the silk panels

Centre each inter-lining side panel piece over a silk lining piece. Mitre the upper corners only, and fold in the upper and side seam allowances, leaving the lower seam allowance open. Carefully press the corners and edges. Stitch the mitres (diag 6).

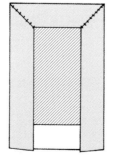

Lace the silk lid lining over the lid lining board in the same manner as the linen base panels.

Constructing the etui base and sides

Using **A** and joining stitch, stitch the lower edge of linen side panel 1 to one edge of the base panel (diag 7).

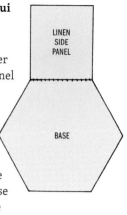

Stitch the lower edge of each remaining linen side panel to the base in order in a clockwise direction in the same manner.

With wrong sides together, align the upper edge of one silk side panel with the upper edge of one linen side panel. Stitch together with joining stitch using the sewing thread. Repeat with the remaining silk and linen side panels (diag 8).

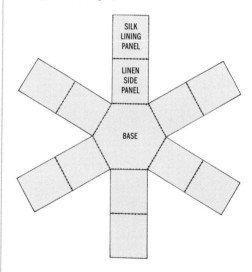

Fold the lining panels to the inside of the side panels. Cut a 46cm (18") length of **L** and press. Thread each end of the ribbon into a tapestry needle.

Hold adjacent long edges of two side panels together, ready to join. Beginning at the base on one side, take one end of the ribbon through the first back stitch on one side panel and the other end through the first back stitch on the second side panel (diag 9).

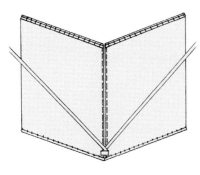

Take care to ensure that the ribbon is centred and remains flat. Working in the same manner as lacing up shoes, cross the ribbons and take them through every second back stitch on opposite sides. Continue working in this manner to the end. After threading the ribbons through the last back stitch on each side, remove the needles and tie the ribbon tails into a bow. Trim away any excess ribbon and cut the tails at a 45 degree angle. Using the sewing thread, work tiny stitches to secure the bow knot. Repeat to join the remaining long edges of the etui side panels, ensuring the loose seam allowances are flat in the base of the etui. If preferred, join the side panels together with joining stitch using **A**.

With the right side uppermost, push the inner base down into the etui.

Constructing the pincushion lid

Fold under a 15mm (⅝") seam allowance on each edge of the silk rectangle and press. Using the sewing thread doubled in the needle and leaving a tail at each end, work a line of gathering 6mm (¼") in from the fold along one long edge.

With the wrong side of the silk hexagon lid panel uppermost, beginning at one corner of the hexagon and using the sewing thread, ladder stitch the long edge of the rectangle without the row of gathering stitch to the hexagon edge. When reaching

the beginning, ladder stitch the two short folded edges of the rectangle together.

Stitch the end of the etui tassel cord to the seam allowance of the silk rectangle upper edge (diag 10).

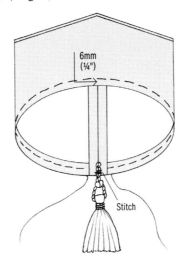

Begin to pull up the gathering threads. Fill the pincushion with fibre-fill and pull up the gathers as tightly as possible. Tie off the gathering threads firmly and trim the tails. There will be a small hole in the centre of the pincushion (diag 11).

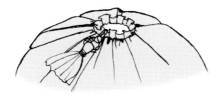

Using the sewing thread, work a line of gathering 6mm (¼") in from the raw edge of the silk circle. Place a 2cm (¾") ball of fiber-fill into the centre of the silk circle and pull up the gathering threads, enclosing the fibre-fill. Tie off the gathering threads (diag 12).

Trim the silk skirt if desired. Push the ball, skirt side down, into the opening in the centre of the pincushion, filling the hole.

Align one edge of the hexagon lid panel with the upper edge of side panel 4. Joining stitch the edges together using the sewing thread.

9. NEEDLEBOOK

Preparing the needlebook

On each linen panel, mitre the corners, fold in the seam allowances and press. Open out the seams and position the interlining inside. Refold the corners and seams. Stitch the mitres. Prepare the silk lining pieces in the same manner. Cut two pieces of green wool felt for the needlebook pages, each 4.5cm x 3cm wide (1 ¾" x 1 ¼"). Centre each felt piece over a silk lining panel. Stitch in place through all layers at each upper corner with a French knot using two strands of **I**.

Constructing the needlebook

With wrong sides together and matching edges, stitch the silk lining panels to the linen panels with joining stitch using the sewing thread, taking care to ensure that the needlepages are correctly aligned.

To make the spine, place the two covers together, linen side outermost, and hold in place with an elastic band so that the edges to be joined are accessible. Cut and press a 56cm (22") length of **L**. Thread each end of the ribbon into a tapestry needle. Beginning at the lower edge, take one end of the ribbon through the first back stitch on the back cover and the other end through the first back stitch on the front cover (diag 13).

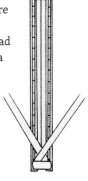

Take care to ensure that the ribbon is centred and remains flat. Working in the same manner as lacing up shoes, cross the ribbons taking them through every back stitch on the opposite sides. Continue working in this manner to the end. After threading the ribbons through the last back stitch on each side, remove the needles and tie the ribbon tails into a bow. Trim away any excess ribbon and cut the tails at a 45 degree angle.

10. SCISSOR SHEATH

Preparing the scissor sheath

On each linen panel, mitre the corners, fold in the seam allowances and press. Open out the seams and position the interlining inside. Refold the corners and seams. Stitch the mitres.

Centre a piece of medium weight fusible interfacing, adhesive side down, over the wrong side of each silk lining piece. Fuse in place.

Position the interlining over the interfacing on the wrong side of one silk piece. Mitre the corners and fold in the seam allowances. Carefully press the corners and edges (diag 14).

Remove the interlining and prepare the remaining silk piece in the same manner. Remove and discard the interlining.

Constructing the scissor sheath

With wrong sides together and aligning the upper edges, position one lining piece over one linen piece. Using the sewing thread, stitch together along the upper edge only with joining stitch.

With linings together and aligning the edges of the linen panels, stitch the front and back together along the side edges and point with joining stitch using **A**.

....

11. SCISSOR FOB

Preparing the scissor fob

On each linen piece mitre the corners, fold in the seam allowance and press. Open out the seams and position the interlining inside. Refold the corners and seams. Trim the seam allowance if necessary and stitch the mitres. Press.

Constructing the scissor fob

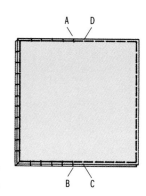

With wrong sides together and matching edges, stitch the fob pieces together with joining stitch between A and B using **A** (diag 15).

Open the panels and place the cord, tassel end down, between them. Close the panels and continue stitching from C to D, taking care not to catch the cord as this will prevent it from sliding. Attach the looped end of the cord to a pair of embroidery scissors.

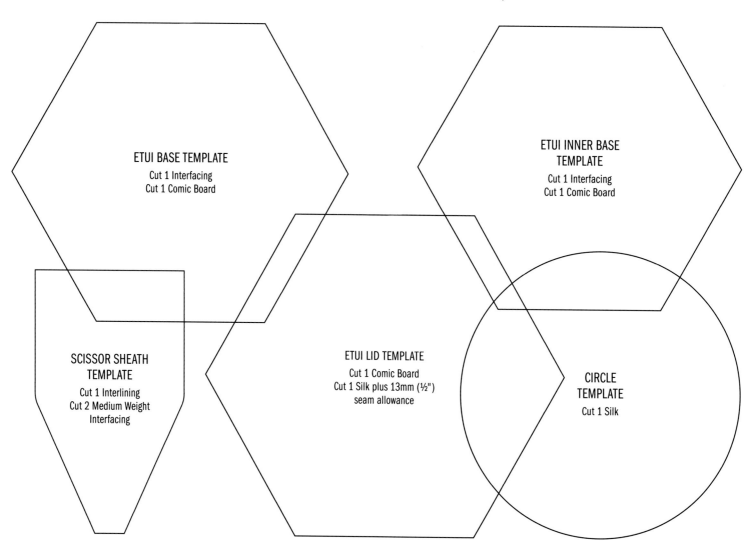

ETUI BASE TEMPLATE
Cut 1 Interfacing
Cut 1 Comic Board

ETUI INNER BASE
TEMPLATE
Cut 1 Interfacing
Cut 1 Comic Board

SCISSOR SHEATH
TEMPLATE
Cut 1 Interlining
Cut 2 Medium Weight
Interfacing

ETUI LID TEMPLATE
Cut 1 Comic Board
Cut 1 Silk plus 13mm (½")
seam allowance

CIRCLE
TEMPLATE
Cut 1 Silk

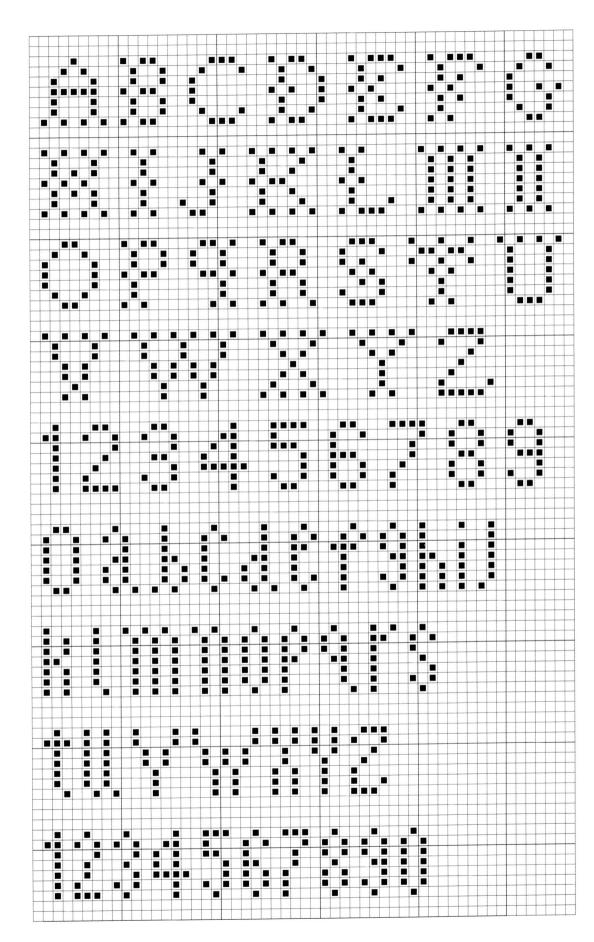

ALPHABET AND NUMBER CHART

BEE CONTAINED ETUI

GATHERING FOR WINTER ETUI

VIRGIN QUEEN'S STITCHING POCKET

BRISTOL BAG ETUI

EXACT CHANGE ETUI

CARDINAL POCKET

TASMANIAN NEEDLE TIDY

ALPHABET AND NUMBER CHART

EXACT CHANGE ETUI

GOOD FOR THE GOOSE BOX

MERMAID BAG ETUI

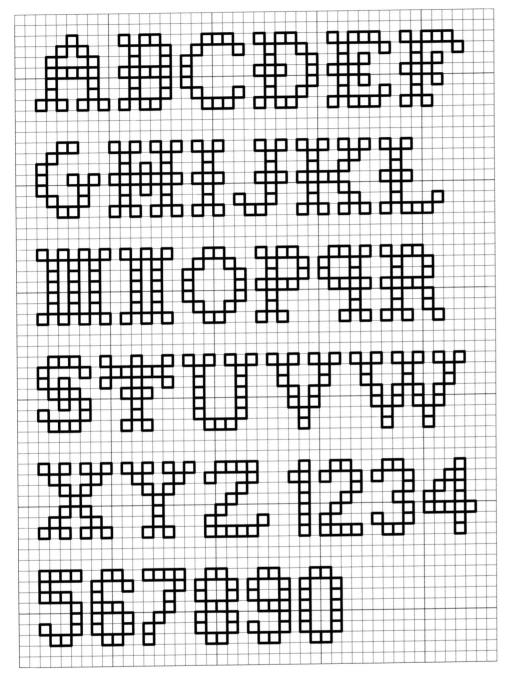

ALPHABET AND NUMBER CHART

HOLBEIN HEXAGON ETUI

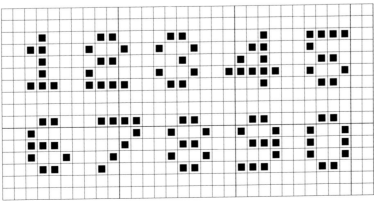

ALPHABET AND NUMBER CHART

GATHERING FOR WINTER ETUI

ACKNOWLEDGEMENTS

I would like to acknowledge the following people for helping me on my needlework journey:

The late Marion Richman, for introducing me to embroidery and giving me my first childhood lessons.

Mari Tutt, for insisting that I purchase a sewing machine and teaching me to make something three-dimensional from a two-dimensional piece of fabric.

The late Betty Flemming, for her support and enthusiasm and for pushing me into the classroom to teach.

Jane Ashbaugh, for the many hours we have shared with needles in our hands and for brain-storming with me on designs and colour palettes.

The members of the Oatlands Chapter of the Embroiderer's Guild of America and The Loudoun Sampler Guild for years of support and guidance.

Maggie Fraser and Lucy Edmison for teaching me to teach embroidery.

My husband, Jim, and my daughter, Caitie, for two decades of support and encouragement. My sister, Anne Brown, for a lifetime of friendship, wonderful times and great advice.

I could keep going but space is limited. So, if I have left you out, please know that I have not forgotten you, I thank you and I hold you in my heart.

Betsy

Thank you, to all the willing hands that made this book possible.

BETSY - your designs have captivated and inspired a generation of stitchers who wholeheartedly embrace and delight in your incredible artisanship. Your generosity and willingness to, once again, invite us into your sewing room and share your heartfelt stories and ensuing designs, are priceless. Thank you!

TEAM INSPIRATIONS - we are continually in awe of your gifts and talents which work together harmoniously to form a creative powerhouse that knows no limits. Your ability to capture the beauty of needlework technically, creativity, figuratively and literally is remarkable. Thank you!

OUR FELLOW STITCHERS – your enthusiasm, encouragement, and appreciation for all we publish is humbling. Willing Hands 2 was produced in direct response to your insatiable appetite and love for all things needle and thread, and in particular, Betsy's stunning work. Never forget how capable and talented your hands are, and may they forever be willing to stitch.

Kristian & Andrea Fleming